Augustus J. C. (Augustus John Cuthbert) Hare

Wanderings in Spain

Augustus J. C. (Augustus John Cuthbert) Hare

Wanderings in Spain

ISBN/EAN: 9783337189747

Printed in Europe, USA, Canada, Australia, Japan

Cover: Foto ©Andreas Hilbeck / pixelio.de

More available books at **www.hansebooks.com**

WANDERINGS IN SPAIN

By AUGUSTUS J. C. HARE
AUTHOR OF "MEMORIALS OF A QUIET LIFE," "WALKS IN ROME," ETC.

WITH SEVENTEEN ILLUSTRATIONS

STRAHAN AND CO.
56, LUDGATE HILL LONDON
1873

[The Right of Translation is Reserved.]

LONDON:
PRINTED BY VIRTUE AND CO.
CITY ROAD.

INTRODUCTION.

THERE are many ways of making a tour in Spain. Of these, the one which is usually chosen is the *comfortable* tour, which takes the traveller by the main line of railway to Madrid, showing him the cathedral of Burgos and the palace of the Escorial on the way, and which carries him on to Toledo, Cordova, Seville, and Granada, almost all places which may be visited and sojourned at with little more of difficulty or of discomfort than is to be met with between London and Paris. The traveller who follows this route generally declines spending his time in stopping at the smaller stations, even though they may be directly on his way; he is content with seing what he has been told is the cream of Spain. But he mnst not imagine that in doing this he has really seen Spain, or that such a tour can give him more than the most cursory glimpse, if as much, into the character and the habits of its people. And even the small benefit and interest which such a traveller might receive on such a journey is barred out from him, if he is hedged in, as is too often the case, by ignorant couriers, or the ciceroni who lurk like bloodthirsty leeches around the doors of the principal hotels.

He who would really see Spain, must go prepared to rough it, must be unembarrassed by a courier (a creature the Spanish mind hates as much as it despises the unfortunate master in leading-strings), must be content with humble inns, coarse fare, windows often glassless, vehicles always jolting, and above all must put all false Anglican pride in his pocket, and treat every Spaniard, from the lowest beggar upwards, as his equal. If he will bear these things, especially if he will unstiffen his English backbone, and genially and cordially respond to the many humble courtesies which he will undoubtedly meet with, he will enjoy Spain, and her abounding treasures of art, of history, of legendary lore, and above all of kindly generous hospitality, will be freely poured out for him. He must take Spain as he finds her; she is not likely to improve; she does not wish to improve; the only way of finding pleasure in her is to take her as she is, without longing for her to be what she is not. The Spanish standard of morals, of manners, of religion, of duty, of all the courtesies which are due from one person to another, however wide apart their rank, is a very different and in most of these points a much higher standard than the English one, and, if an English traveller will not at least endeavour to come up to it, he had much better stay at home.

It is also necessary at once to lay aside all false expectations as to what one will find. Spain is *not* a beautiful country. If a traveller expects to find the soft charm and luxuriant loveliness of Italy, life in Spain will be a constant disappointment: no hope can possibly be more misplaced. Spain is not the least like Italy: it has not even the beauty of the greater part of France. Beyond the Asturias and the valleys near the Pyrenees, there is not a tree worth speaking of in the Peninsula. There is scarcely any grass; the shrubs may even be counted; except when the corn is out, which here lasts such a short time, there is hardly any vegetation at all. Those who wish to find beauty must only look for beauty of an especial kind—without verdure, or refinement, or colour. But the artist will be satisfied without these, and will exult in the long lines, in the unbroken expanses of the stony, treeless, desolate sierras, while every crevice of the distant hills is distinctly visible in the transparent atmosphere, and the shadows of the clouds fall blue upon the pale yellow of the tawny desert. In the central provinces, hundreds and hundreds of miles may be traversed, and no single feature of striking natural beauty be met with; nothing more than the picturesque effects which may always be obtained by the groups of cattle, gathered round fountains by the dusty wayside or standing out as if embossed against the pale distances, or by the long trains of mules with their drivers in brigand-like costume and flowing *mantas* bearing merchandise from one town to another. On these plains, too, there is a silence which is almost ghastly, for there are no singing birds, scarcely even any insects. Such is the character of almost all the country now traversed by the principal railways, which was formerly toiled through in diligence or on mule-back. But even here, just when the spirits begin to flag, and the wearied eye longs to refresh itself, the traveller reaches one of the grand old cities which seem to have gone to sleep for five hundred years and to have scarcely waked up again, where you step at once out of the reign of Amadeo or Isabella II. into that of Philip II., and find the buildings, the costumes, the proverbs, the habits, the daily life, those of his time. You wonder what Spain has been doing since, and the answer is quite easy—nothing. It has not the slightest wish to do anything more; it is quite satisfied. The Catholic sovereigns Ferdinand and Isabella made a great nation of it, and filled it with glorious works. Since then it has had, well—reverses, but it has changed as little as ever it could. It has delighted in its conservatism in everything, down to the sleepy wickedness of its Bourbon sovereigns. We said to many a Spaniard who lamented over the absence of Isabella, "Oh, but she was so dreadfully wicked." "Ah, yes," was the answer, with a look of much sympathy for the exile, "she had indeed all the dear old Spanish vices." And for the sake of those ancestral vices even, many will not rest till they have her back again.

How the Spaniards hate and abuse the railways, though they use them! Certainly they make them go as slow as possible, and bring the trains as nearly as possible to the speed of the old mule-traffic. And as for carriages in country places, they are little more than a square of bars with ropes between, through which you tumble, and stick, and flounder as best you may, while you are being furiously jolted over the rugged, rutty, rocky roads.

Except in the Asturias and some parts of Galicia, I am only aware of two places where there is anything that may be called beautiful *country* in Spain, and these are Monserrat, the noblest, the most gloriously beautiful of rocks, and the palm-groves of Elche. The latter is indeed quite surpassingly beautiful, and a painter might linger for ever upon the glowing loveliness of its contrasts, where the stony yellow plain sweeps up close with the luxuriant palm-woods. It has more of the ideal Africa than Africa itself, and is the most splendid oasis in a singularly dismal desert. Generally, African travellers complain of the Spanish deserts as being deserts without any oases at all.

Travel in Spain then becomes a constant movement from one town to another—towns which are not as beautiful as those in Italy, not as picturesque as many of those in France and Germany, but which have a peculiar charm of their own in their tortuous whitewashed streets, their vast brown mouldering palaces, and their colossal churches, which nothing but sight can give the impression of. Such a town Kenelm Digby describes when he wishes that his "Broadstone of Honour" may resemble "one of those beautiful old cities in Spain, in which one finds everything; cool walks shaded by orange-trees along the banks of a river; great open squares exposed to the burning sun, for festivities; narrow, winding, dark streets, composed of houses of every form, height, age, colour; labyrinths of buildings, all confused together, palaces, hospitals, convents, halls, all raised in an appropriate style of architecture; market-places, resounding to the busy hum of men; cemeteries, where the living are as silent as the dead; in the centre, the vast gothic cathedral, with its airy spires and massive tower, its fine sculptured portals, and its arches and capitals of varied tracery, its deep vaults, its forests of pillars, its burning chapels, its multitude of saints, its high altar lighted with a thousand tapers—wonderful structure! imposing by its enormous magnitude, curious in its details, sublime when seen from a distance of two leagues, and beautiful when only two paces from the eye. Then, in another quarter of the city, the vast arch or aqueduct, constructed by the

Romans, or, concealed by a grove of palms and sycamore, the ruins of the Oriental mosque, with its domes of brass and enamelled pavements."

Such a town as this is Salamanca on the beautiful Tormes; such is Segovia, with its richly decorated streets, its wide views over the wild surrounding sierras, and its deep green gorges filled with old churches and convents. Such, above all, is Granada, the climax of the beauty and interest of Spain, a place which alone is worth all and tenfold the fatigue and trouble which may be undertaken to reach it. Long before railway days, I knew some ladies, who being delayed for a few days between two steamers at Malaga, determined to reach Granada, though it was only possible to spend one day there. Day and night, though in feeble health, they rode on in ever-increasing exhaustion. At last, on the summit of a desolate mountain, their strength altogether gave way, and they felt it impossible to proceed further. But just then, a solitary traveller approached from the other side of the pass—the path was so narrow, so hemmed in by precipices, that it was impossible to linger—there was no time for many words, but as the stranger passed, he exclaimed, "Go on, go on, it is alike the Paradise of Nature and of Art,"—and they took courage and went on, and found it, as so many thousands of travellers have done since, the most perfectly beautiful place in the world.

There is no mine of interest which has been less explored than that of Spain. Singularly little has been written about it, even in its own language. The traveller's library need not be very large. There is no book like Ford, which cannot be done without, but then it must be the old original undistorted edition, which is now very difficult to procure. O'Shea is a capital guide-book for the commonly visited places, has more correct recent information than Murray, from which it differs entirely both in plan and material, and is the best for practical purposes. The volume of Kugler's Handbook, on the Spanish Schools of Painting, may be found useful in the galleries of Valencia, Seville, and Madrid, though most of its information is given in a more agreeable and attention-arresting form in a charming volume called "Spanish Towns and Spanish Pictures," by Mrs. W. A. Tollemache. Street's ponderous volume on the "Gothic Architecture of Spain" may be instructively studied for the churches of the north before leaving home. Hans Christian

Andersen's vivid sketches "In Spain" are pleasant reading upon the spot, and in French the admirable "Voyage en Espagne" of Théophile Gautier. But if one goes beyond mere architecture and picture-seeing, into that which makes Spain what it is, the living, active—or rather the dead, inactive—pulse of its people, filled with poetical thoughts, existing in an atmosphere of semi-Eastern imagery, which flows in songs and proverbs from their lips, there are a series of modern Spanish romances, giving an unexaggerated picture of the life and character of the people, which should indeed be more carefully studied than any hand-book, and which are the pleasantest of companions in the long weary railway journeys, which offer nothing to see and very little to think about. Perfectly charming are the little novels and poems of Gustave Becquer, the historical tales of Trueba, the poems of Don Melchor de Palau—but above all the inexhaustible wealth of beautiful word-pictures which may be enjoyed in the stories of Fernan Caballero, which collect so much, and reveal so much, and teach so much, that it is scarcely possible sufficiently to express one's obligation to them.

Tired of modern novels, a traveller, who has

taken the trouble to make some acquaintance with the language, may be curious to know at least the names and characteristics of those who have used it with the greatest success, for, with the single exception of Don Quixote, Spanish authors are but little known beyond the Peninsula. Graver students may be referred at once to the " Literary Histories" of Bouterwek (tr. by Th. Ross) and Ticknor.

The earliest monument of Spanish literature (it is also the earliest epic in any modern language) is the rhymed chronicle known as the "Poem of the Cid." The hero's exile and return, his conquest of Valencia, the marriage of his daughters with the Infants of Carrion, the cruel treatment they suffer from their husbands, and their re-marriage with the Infants of Navarre and Arragon, are the events told naively in these rude verses. The Cid died in 1099, and the poem may date some fifty years later. The ordinary reader will get an ample idea of its gist and spirit in the admirable translations of John Hookham Frere (in his collected works, vol. ii., pp. 411—437).

After "The Cid" follow the rhymed tales of the Romancero and Cancionero-General, and the many volumes of romances and stories of knight-errantry so lovingly collected and studied by Don Quixote, and of which the curé and the barber made so ruthless a holocaust.

All but antiquaries, however, will skip at once from the age of Ruy Diaz to that of Charles V., when a new race of poets began to seek their inspiration from classical and Italian sources; when Virgil, Horace, and Petrarch were studied and imitated, and the Italian sonnet and canzone were acclimatised in Spain. Copious stores of lyric and pastoral poetry still survive to keep fresh in Spain the names of Boscan, Garcilaso, Mendoza, Herrera, and Luis de Leon. At last (1547—1616) appeared Cervantes. Don Quixote needs no word of comment, but the reader may perhaps be reminded that to the same pen Spain owes some capital stories, somewhat in the style of Boccaccio (the Novelas Ejemplares), and an admirable tragedy, "Numantia." The great outburst of Spanish genius extends (just as in Greece and England) through a period of little more than a century, contained within the reigns of Philip II., III., IV. What the Persian War was to the Greek, the discovery and conquest of the New World was to the Spaniard; and in the lull which followed either event the passionate attachment to the altars and homes of their fatherland, and the lofty pride in their history, which filled every breast in both nations, found its highest expression in the drama. Lope de Vega (1562—1635), who is said to have written nearly two thousand plays, stands first in fertility and inventive genius; Calderon (1600—1681) in wealth of imagery, and deep religious feeling. In his power of portraying the most tender "sensibility of principle," the most perfect "chastity of honour," Calderon stands alone among poets. Englishmen will do well to approach this singular genius through the graceful essay of Archbishop Trench, and the fragmentary translation of the Magico Prodigioso by Shelley.

So far the great charm of Spanish literature lay in the fact that its *chefs-d'œuvre* were less mannered and learned, and more original and national than those of other countries. But before the death of Lope de Vega a new school had arisen which affected a superlative purity of expression and style. Ample specimens of its versatile founder Gongora (1561—1627), and an interesting account of the controversies his works provoked may be found in an essay by Archdeacon Churton entitled "Gongora."

A beginner will find his best help to the language in Del Mar's Grammar, and Neuman and Baretti's

Dictionary; with these at his side let him begin by attacking Padre Isla's translation of Gil Blas or one of Fernan Caballero's novelettes.

Spain is now so encircled by railways that almost everything of importance may be visited by rail. The following is the tour we intended to make, though we were prevented ultimately from accomplishing a part of it, and it embraces all the principal objects of interest in Spain and Portugal.

IRUN (excursion in carriage to Fontarabia).
S. SEBASTIAN.
PAMPLONA (ride to Roncesvalles).
TUDELA (visit—by carriage—Tarragona, and—on mules—Veruela).
TAFALLA AND OLITE.
ZARAGOZA.
HUESCA (walk or ride to visit the neighbouring convents).
LERIDA.
MANRESA (drive to the curious mines of Cardoña).
MONISTROL (walk or drive to Monserrat, and remain some days at the convent, seeing the neighbourhood on foot).
BARCELONA (visit Pedralles, and San Culgat del Vallis—going by rail to Serdanola and walking from thence).
RIPOLL, rail and drive.
GERONA.
MARTORELL.
TARRAGONA (visit Poblet and other monasteries, taking the railway to Montblanch, and driving or walking from thence).
SAGUNTUM.
VALENCIA.
JATIVA.
ALICANTE, hence drive to—
ELCHE, drive to—

ORIHUELA, and on to—
MURCIA.
CORDOVA (ride or walk to the hermitages of Val Paraiso).
SEVILLE (drive to Italica).
XERES.
CADIZ, whence by sea, or ride by Tarifa, to—
ALGECIRAS, steamer to—
GIBRALTAR, and on mules to—
RONDA, whence ride and rail to—
MALAGA, or direct to—
GRANADA (excursion to the Alpuxarras and Alhama), diligence to—
JAEN, and on to Menzibar, whence by rail to—
MERIDA.
SANTAREM.
LISBON (excursion to Cintra and Mafra), by rail to Carregado and carriage, by Caldas da Rainha, to—
ALCOBAÇA, and on to—
BATALHA, and on to—
COIMBRA.
OPORTO, carriage or sea to—
VIGO, carriage to—
SANTIAGO, diligence to—
LUGO, and to—
VILLA FRANCA DEL VIERZO (whence ride or walk to the monasteries), and carriage to—
ASTORGA.
LEON, diligence to—
OVIEDO, ride to—
COVADONGA, and ride on to—
SANTANDER.
PALENCIA.
ZAMORA, diligence to—
SALAMANCA, diligence to—
AVILA.
MADRID.

TOLEDO.
ARANJUEZ, and return to—
MADRID (excursion by rail to Alcala, Guadalajara and Siguenza).
VILALBA, diligence to La Granja and diligence or carriage to—
SEGOVIA, diligence back to Vilalba and rail to—
ESCORIAL.
VALLADOLID (drive to the Tower of Simancas).
BURGOS (drive to Miraflores and S. Pedro de Cerdeña).
IRUN.

As a certain degree of physical well-being is quite essential to mental enjoyment, a Spanish traveller who intends to visit obscure places should certainly not set out unprovided with some of the comforts of life—some tea, Liebig's soup, soap, and a few common medicines should on no account be left behind. It should also be remembered, that except in the extreme south, and on part of the east coast, the cold in Spain is quite as severe, or more so, than in the north of Europe—though it is a dry healthy cold—and a good supply of warm wraps must be provided.

Spanish "Travellers' Rests" are of three kinds:—a *Fonda*, which answers to an hotel; a *Posada*, which represents an inn, though generally of very inferior quality; and a *Venta*, which is the merest public-house. In almost all the towns, however, are *Casas de Huespedes*, boarding houses, where food and lodging are supplied at a fixed price, and which, as regards the latter, are often very comfortable; of the former it is seldom that much can be said. Houses of this kind which have rooms to be let furnished, hang out a piece of white paper from the *middle* of their balcony, but when the rooms are unfurnished, the paper is placed at the corner of the balcony. Almost all Spanish houses are distinguished by a heavy shield or coat-of-arms, often of very curious historical origin. Such is the badge of " El Nodo " represented on the outside of this volume, which is borne proudly over the gates of Seville and its Alcazar, given by Alonzo el Sabio, when that town alone was faithful to him in his misfortunes, and meaning " No m'ha dejado " ("She has not deserted me"), *Madeja* being expressed by the central figure representing *a skein*.

CONTENTS.

		PAGE
I.	NAVARRE AND ARRAGON	1
II.	IN CATALONIA	21
III.	BARCELONA AND GERONA	38
IV.	TARRAGONA AND POBLET	50
V.	VALENCIA, ALICANTE, AND ELCHE	66
VI.	CORDOVA	85
VII.	SEVILLE	93
VIII.	CADIZ AND GIBRALTAR	129
IX.	GRANADA	137
X.	ARANJUEZ AND TOLEDO	173
XI.	MADRID AND THE ESCORIAL	200
XII.	SEGOVIA AND AVILA	229
XIII.	SALAMANCA, VALLADOLID, AND BURGOS	254

LIST OF ILLUSTRATIONS.

	PAGE
TOLEDO	*Frontispiece.*
LERIDA	*to face page* 22
BARCELONA	38
CATHEDRAL, TARRAGONA	52
CASTLE OF ALICANTE	77
AT ELCHE	80
CORDOVA	86
SEVILLE	96
GIBRALTAR FROM ALGECIRAS	132
GATE OF JUSTICE, ALHAMBRA	142
COURT OF BLESSING, ALHAMBRA	150
PUERTA DEL SOL, TOLEDO	180
STATUE OF PHILIP IV., MADRID	208
SEGOVIA	230
PALACE OF LA GRANJA	238
SALAMANCA	256
ARCO DE SANCTA MARIA, BURGOS	268

I.

NAVARRE AND ARRAGON.

ZARAGOZA, *December* 29, 1871.

WE have entered Spain at the end of December, which is by no means the best time of the year for beginning our tour. The traveller who intends to make a long progress through the Peninsula, and who wishes to do it comfortably and pleasantly, should not set out later than October, when he may hope to pass through one side of the bleak northern provinces, and reach beauty and sunshine before the cold weather sets in. In this we were prevented, but we have begun our journey, determined to find all possible compensation for our fatigues, to look at the bright side in everything, and, above all, not to be deterred by a little difficulty from seeing all we have come to visit.

Our passage of the boundary-line between

France and Spain was by no means triumphant. Just at the critical moment, when we were about to cross the Bidassoa, and all heads were out of the windows watching for the famous Isle of Pheasants, crash went the train off the line, knocking everybody back into their seats, and swamping sentiment in fright. We seemed likely to be detained for hours, but there is wonderful strength in numbers, and such a multitude of peasants obeyed the summons to assist in lifting the refractory carriages on to the line again, that less than an hour saw them all replaced, and five minutes after, we steamed across the narrow channel and entered Spain.

The change on crossing the boundary is strangely instantaneous, and the traveller is forced at once to realise how impossible it will be to travel in Spain without at least some knowledge of its language; for even on the frontier no other is understood, and the most embarrassing confusion is also in store for one who has not already mastered the intricate varieties of the Spanish coinage in which his fresh tickets have to be paid for. Immediately, also, Spanish customs come into play. You ask his worship the Porter to have the graciousness to assist you in lifting your portmanteau ("Mozo, hágame Usted el favor de llevar mi maleta"), and you implore his worship the Beggar, your brother, for the love of God to excuse you from giving him anything ("Perdóneme Usted, por Dios, hermano"). Pleasantly, however, does this excess of Spanish courtesy strike you when you are about to enter the railway carriage. However crowded it may be already, however filled up with the hand-bags and other impedimenta of its occupants, the new-comers, who would be scowled upon in England, are welcomed with smiles and willing help; places are at once made for them, their bags and baskets are comfortably stowed away, and everything that can be supplied is offered for their convenience; every Spanish gentleman is willing to assist, translate, or advise; and if you travel in the second-class carriages, which, as in many parts of Germany, are, in the north of Spain, often much more roomy and comfortable, and generally far less crowded than the first, not even the humblest peasant leaves it without lifting his hat and wishing you a hearty "A Dios, Señores."

The train crawls along in the most provoking way, stopping at all the small stations for two, four, ten, twenty minutes, and giving you ample time to survey the scenery. You feel impatient, but your Spanish companions are perfectly satisfied, "it is so much safer, so satisfactory never to have any accidents." Time is of no importance to them whatever. "One can smoke one's cigarritos as well in one place as another." This *insouciance* was fully displayed when we reached the junction station of Alsasua, where we were to change for Pamplona, and found our train had just been taken off by the company, without any previous notice having been given to that effect. It was pitch dark, and from the pouring rain which had continued for several days, the wild country round was little better than a swamp, so the prospect of a whole day's detention was by no means exhilarating; but finding our Spanish friends received the announcement with no greater expression of displeasure than a shrug of the shoulders, we thought it better to take it in the same way, and, as they said, to "avoid the fatigue of discomposing ourselves." Lanterns were brought to guide us down a slippery causeway and through a slough of red mud to a humble cottage-like Posada, where a woman with her head tied up in a bright red-and-yellow handkerchief gave us a warm reception, surrounded by her five cats and as many children. We found everything much better than we had expected; the small bedrooms had clean boarded floors, though no more furniture than was absolutely necessary, and the straw mattresses were covered with clean linen. There were no fire-places, but during the evening each was warmed for a time with a brasero filled with smouldering wood ashes. The night was bitterly cold, for the hills close around were thickly covered with snow; and after a humble supper of broth, boiled eggs, and potatoes, we clustered round a log-fire in the lower room, our party being increased by the station-master and two travelling bagmen, who diverted us with their various experiences, while the cats fought and screeched in the background. In the morning a small cup of chocolate was served to each, with some dry bread, for we had taken leave of butter on taking leave of the French soil. The hours of waiting passed more quickly than we expected, and the following afternoon we were speeding through the bleak mountainous country, interspersed with oak and cork woods.

Long before we reached it, we could see the rock-built Pamplona, its brown towers and walls standing out as if embossed against the delicate pale pink of the snow-tipped mountains, and rising from the long reaches of the dead green Cuenca, as the surrounding plain is called, the cup which contains the precious "key of Navarre," and which here closely resembles the Roman Campagna in its desolation and colouring.

The station is deep in the valley, and an omnibus took us into the town by a steep winding road, skirting the high walls, and passing a drawbridge and gateway. The only trees to be seen were a few white poplars, allowed to linger in life, when all other trees are cut down, in regard to the old Spanish belief that they were the first trees the Almighty created—the Adam of vegetation.

On entering the town the aspect of things is thoroughly Spanish: the brightly-painted houses thickly hung with balconies of wrought ironwork; the small "plazas" with their grey churches, in front of which groups of priests are seen mingling with the gay costumes of the peasantry; the great square surrounded by its heavy arcades; the avenues and gardens, especially that known as "La Taconera," the favourite resort of handsome black-robed señoras in their flowing mantillas, for here, indeed, a bonnet is unknown, and its wearer is followed about and pointed at as a curiosity.

From the great Plaza, considered to be one of the largest in Spain, in which 10,000 Jews were burnt alive to do honour to the marriage of a Count de Champagne—a human bonfire, which was visible from all the country round—a steep, stony street leads to the cathedral. Its Ionic front, built by Ventura Rodriquez in 1780, causes one to be agreeably surprised with the rest of the building, which dates from 1397, when Charles the Noble (or III.) pulled down an older church of 1100, leaving only the chapter-house and a part of the cloisters.

In the interior the tourist will first see the peculiar arrangement which is usual in the Spanish churches. Far down the nave, almost to its last pier, extends the raised *coro*, used only by the canons and choristers, and entirely shut in by its high partition walls, except where, towards the east, a passage marked by low brass rails (*rejas*), to prevent the priests from being pressed upon by the people, leads to the high altar, where the huge and splendid carved altar-piece, known as a *retablo*, takes the place of the reredos of an English cathedral. At the east end of the coro is the magnificent tomb of the founder, with his figure and that of his queen Leonor. The cloisters, enclosing a tangled garden and a lonely cypress, are a perfect dream of beauty, each canopied arch rising against the light open gallery of the second story, so as to display its delicate stonework to perfection. Here among other curiosities, is the tomb of Miguel Ancheta, sculptor of the choir stall-work, with a curious epitaph, and a little chapel enclosed by an iron palisade made from the chains taken in the battle of Las Navas de Tolosa. The knocker of the north transept door, formed by two serpents, is another noteworthy piece of ancient ironwork.

From the cathedral we follow the line of the walls—whose strength in the middle ages gave Pamplona the title of "muy noble, muy leal, y muy heroica," and which are said to have been originally founded by the sons of Pompey, who called the place Pompeiopolis,—till we emerged upon the Taconera, close to the church of S. Lorenzo, which contains a statue of the tutelar saint of the city, St. Fermin, who was born at Pamplona, but afterwards went to preach at Amiens, where his miracles are carved around the choir, and where the delicious scent of his dead body revealed its resting-place to the bishop, —his disinterment in mid winter being celebrated by an entire resurrection of nature, and the recovery of all the sick.

Near this is the citadel, which was besieged in 1521 by the army of Francis I., while Charles V. was absent in Germany. A handsome young knight, Ignatius Loyola, had been left to guard it, and defended it bravely, but was wounded and disabled, and the garrison surrendered upon seeing him fall. A cannon-ball had struck Loyola on both legs, and such was his personal vanity, that he insisted, after the wounds were healed, upon having his legs twice opened, and a projecting bone sawn off, lest their appearance should be injured; all, however, was of no avail, and he was lame for life. During his detention in the castle of Loyola, he asked for romances to amuse his convalescence, and none being forthcoming, lives of our Saviour and the saints were brought to him, which made him say to himself—" These men were of the same frame as I am, why should I not do as they have done?"—and he rose from his sick-bed with a firm desire to imitate them and to abandon the world and its vanities. The fair lady, to whom he declared that he would henceforth devote himself as champion, was the Virgin Mother of God, and the wars he would wage were those against the spiritual enemies of God's people. This change in the life of the founder of the Jesuits is commemorated at Pamplona by a small chapel near one of the gates, which contains an interesting portrait of Loyola, in his soldier's dress.

The Christmas mass in the cathedral of Pamplona was magnificent. No service in Italy can compare with the solemn bursts of music which follow the thrilling solos sung in these old Spanish churches, where every possible instrument is pressed into the service of the orchestra; and not less striking is the effect of the multitude of veiled figures who kneel in the dim light between the coro and the altar. At the *table d'hôte*, in honour of the day, we are regaled with *turroncs*, a kind of almond hard-bake, only produced at Christmas.

A dreary journey, through a dismal barren wilderness, brought us to Tudela. On the way we passed Tafalla and Olite, once called the "Flowers of Navarre," and both of them royal residences, but now squalid villages of miserable hovels. In Olite, however, are two fine parish churches, and considerable remains of the ancient palace, which would be quite worth stopping at, and sketching between two trains, in fine weather, though the miserable town has no accomodation for travellers.

It was late and quite dark on Christmas Day when we reached Tudela and took a boy to guide us through the frozen streets to the Fonda della Caravaca. The cold was pitiless, and in our barely furnished rooms above a stable, without fire-places or even a brasero, it was impossible to obtain any warmth at all. Tudela does not, we think, deserve the praise Street bestows upon it, as containing "a church which is to be classed among the very best in any part of Europe," though the round-arched doors of the transepts are very grand, and that at the west end, of enormous span, encrusted all over with sculpture, is absolutely magnificent. I say round-arched advisedly, this style in Spain being more properly known as Gothic, while Pointed is spoken of as the German style. One descends a flight of steps from the west door into the church, which is greatly bedaubed all over and spoilt by grey and white paint. Similarly injured and much built up are the cloisters, which were exhibited to us, with some pride, by the priests of the church, from whom here, as everywhere in Spain, we experienced the greatest kindness and civility. A tower near the church,—which is a *parroquia*, not a cathedral,—has the picturesque Moorish decoration of coloured tiles inlaid in patterns.

In the evening we crossed the long narrow bridge of seventeen arches, and found a pleasant sunny walk by the banks of the Ebro, which is as yellow as the Tiber. But the fierce cold prevented our making the interesting excursion by diligence to Tarragona, and riding from thence on mules up the mountains to the abbey of Veruela, the oldest Cistercian house in Spain. Those who read as we have done the beautiful letters of Gustavo Becquer, written 'Desde mi Celda,' in this convent, and filled with the most lovely pictures of nature amid its surrounding scenery, will long to visit the spot whence they were drawn.

To do justice to the ugliness of the scenery between Tudela and Zaragoza would be impossible—to the utter desolation of the treeless, stony, uninhabited wastes, across which the ice-laden north-west winds whistle uninterruptedly. But at length the railway skirts the Ebro, and almost immediately passes the grand old bridge built in 1437, beyond which, on either side of the principal thoroughfare, rise the two cathedrals of Zaragoza, in which the chapter does duty for six months alternately. Through narrow, squalid streets an omnibus takes you to the broad open Plaza de la Constitucion, where the comfortable Fonda de Europa is situated. In this, as in all other Spanish hotels, a fixed price exists, which includes apartments, food—at the regular meals provided by the hotel—service, and lights. No extra charges are made. The cost of living in these hotels varies from the equivalent of five to eight shillings, generally in proportion to the importance of the place where you may be.

In the older Spanish towns it is useless to take a guide, and it is almost equally so to ask your way, as the natives are wholly unacquainted with their own antiquities, and uninstructed in their own history. It is only to those who wander indefatigably through the winding streets, that all the interesting objects gradually reveal themselves, though the process is often assisted by the ascent, in the first instance, of some lofty tower, whence the town is seen as in a map.

At Zaragoza the sights naturally begin with the bridge, to the left of which rises the older cathedral of El Seo. Its front, modernised in the seventeenth century, occupies one side of a square, which also contains the archiepiscopal palace and the Lonja, or exchange, a fine but decaying building of 1551, with a richly carved projecting soffit, beneath which many heads of kings and knights are inserted in medallion frames. The north-east wall and apse of the church are splendid specimens of mauresque diaper-work, inlaid with coloured tiles.

On entering the cathedral from the sunlit square, one finds oneself in absolute darkness until one's eyes become accustomed to the change, so intense is the gloom which reigns amid its solemn Gothic arches, where even the faint light from the small round windows high up in the walls is tempered by crimson curtains. Besides these there are no other windows in the body of the church, the whole face of the lower walls being filled up with a mass of Churriguerresque sculpture (so called from the much-abused architect, José Churriguerra, who died 1725), which, though paltry and tasteless in detail, is inexpressibly rich and gorgeous in its general effect. The centre of the five aisles is occupied by the coro, surrounded by a magnificent screen, incrusted with statues and bas-reliefs, which tell the stories of San Lorenzo and San Vicente. At its western extremity, or *trascoro*, a statue of Canon Funes kneels in a niche, on the selfsame spot where he is supposed to have knelt in his lifetime, when conversing with the Virgin. No low rejas, as at Pamplona, lead from the coro to the high altar, which only slightly recedes from beneath the beautiful lanthorn-tower, or *Cimborio*, of 1520. Over the altar is a vast retablo, around which are grouped the tombs of several sixteenth-century archbishops, and that of the heart of Don Balthazar, son of Philip IV., the well-known Infante of Velasquez, who died here of the small-pox, at the age of seventeen. On the right of the altar is a grand plateresque door leading to the sacristy, and near it a chapel commemorating the so-called martyrdom of the fierce inquisitor San Pedro Arbues, who shared the fate of Thomas à Becket, being murdered in this cathedral by Vidal Duranso, September 15, 1495. He well deserved this end for his cruelties, and it has been of the utmost service to art, in giving rise to one of the finest pictures of Murillo, a pendant to the St. Peter Martyr of Titian. Tradition says that, on his assassination, the great bell of Velilla was heard to strike, being the fourth time since the Moorish occupation; its miraculous tolling always announcing some disaster to the monarchy. At the west end of the church is a chapel containing the tombs of Archbishop Fernando, grandson of Ferdinand the Catholic, and his mother, Aña Gurrea, by the admirable sculptor Diego Morlanes.

Leaving the Seo, the traveller should cross to the other cathedral of El Pilar, than which it is impossible to imagine a more complete contrast. Outside, it resembles a mosque, or Sant' Antonio of Padua, in its endless towers and domes, covered with bright orange, green, and blue tiles, which glitter in the sunshine. Though much modernised in the last century, the exterior of the building, five hundred feet in length, is imposing from its vast size. Within, it is a monument of folly and bad taste, painted and gilt like a Parisian café. Towards its western extremity, in the centre of the nave, is the *sanctum sanctorum*, a semi-circular temple, surrounded by granite columns, where the Virgin, descending upon a pillar, part of which may be seen through a hole—it is too sacred to be gazed upon in its entirety—appeared to Santiago.

This famous shrine, which had its origin in Arragonese jealousy of the pilgrimages to the Castilian Compostella, is one of the greatest loadstars of Spanish devotion. Hundreds of pilgrims are always kneeling in front of the black image, or pressing to kiss its feet. The wardrobe of La Virgen del Pilar is inexhaustible, and she is constantly changing her gorgeous apparel, the priests who perform her toilette averting their eyes at the time, lest they should be struck with blindness by the contemplation of her charms. Fifty thousand pilgrims sometimes flock hither on the 12th of October alone, which is the festival of the Pilar; and no wonder, for "God alone," said Pope Innocent III., "can count the miracles which are then performed here;" while Cardinal Retz, who was here in 1649, affirms in his memoirs, that he saw with his own eyes a leg which had been cut off grow again upon being rubbed with oil from one of the Virgin's lamps.

In the Calle Santiago, near El Pilar, is one of the best specimens of an old Zaragozan house, enclosing a patio, or courtyard, surrounded with sculptured pillars, but now decaying, like everything here (except idol-worship), and turned into a coach-maker's yard. Hence, as well as the inexhaustible and interminable beggars would allow, we followed the narrow streets to the Plaza San Felipe, which contains the leaning tower of Spain—the grand octangular Torre Nueva, diapered all over with lace-like patterns from Moorish designs.

A neighbouring church, San Pablo, is a most picturesque relic of the thirteenth century, with a fine retablo by Damian Forment of Valencia, a coro of 1500, and another splendid octagonal brick tower. Hard by is the site of the Portillo, where Agostina, the maid of Zaragoza, snatched the match from the hand of her slaughtered lover and worked the gun in his place. Enclosed in a barrack near this are some decaying remains of the Moorish palace, Aljaferia.

We re-entered the town by the handsome promenade called Paseo de Santa Engracia, from a fine church which was completed by Charles V. All except the west front was destroyed by the French in 1808, but this, with its portal in the form of a retablo, is well worth examination, being filled with delicate sculpture of 1505 by Juan Morlanes. Gerónimo Zurita, the famous historian of Arragon, died and was buried in this convent, 1580. A little farther than this, on the line of the city wall, is San Miguel, perhaps the richest, as it is the most picturesque, of all the fifteenth century buildings of Zaragoza, covered with delicate Moorish tracery. All these would be most delightful and interesting, but in these fierce ice-laden winds it is almost impossible to look at them without feeling cut to pieces. Blocks of ice line the streets, and the miserable plants on the public walks are shrivelled up and blackened in their vases. People are walking about wrapped in huge *mantas* like blankets, which cover their heads and bodies at the same time: and now, in front of the hotel, a poor woman shivering with cold, though enveloped in a manta of gorgeous colours, is trying to earn a few cuartos by singing snatches from the song of the season, the strange but wonderfully picturesque "Noche Buena." Here are some of them:—

> "La Virgen se fué á lavar
> Sus manos blancas al rio;
> El sol se quedó parado,
> La mar perdió su ruido.

> "Los pastores de Belen
> Todos juntos van por leña,
> Para calentar al niño
> Que nació la noche buena.
> * * *

> "San José era carpintero,
> Y la Virgen costurera
> Y el niño labra la Cruz
> Por que ha de morir en ella"—

which may be rendered thus:—

> "To the stream the Virgin Mother
> Hied, her fair white hands to lave:
> The wond'ring sun stood still in heaven;
> And ocean hushed his rolling wave.

"One and all came Bethlehem's shepherds,
   Fuel-laden from the height,
Warmth to bring the Blessed Nursling,
   Who was born that happy night.

   *   *   *   *   *

"A carpenter was good St. Joseph,
   A seamstress poor the mother maid;
The Child it toiled the cross to fashion.
   On which our ransom should be paid."

II.

IN CATALONIA.

Convent of Monserrat, *January* 4, 1872.

HIDEOUS as was the country we had passed through before reaching Zaragoza, it paled before the frightfulness of that which we had to traverse on the way to Lerida—six hours without a tree or shrub or symptom of vegetation, but barren, malaria-stricken swamps, riven here and there into deep crevasses by the action of some extinct volcano, seeming alike forsaken by God and man. From Tardienta, a branch railway leads to Huesca, which is exceedingly worth visiting, as well for the sake of the relics it contains of the old palace of the Arragonese kings, as for the number of curious churches and convents scattered over the surrounding hills, which have never been sufficiently explored by English travellers. But the cold was still so severe, and the rain falling in such torrents, that we thought it safer to proceed at once to Lerida, where we knew we should find better accommodation, and where we had been told that the climate would begin to be milder.

It was not until we reached our destination that the scenery began to improve; but Lerida looks down upon an olive-clad plain, and in itself is gloriously picturesque, a huge mass of purple rock, three hundred feet high, being crowned by fortifications containing the old cathedral, with its tall tower and long line of cloister arches rising from the very edge of the precipice. The narrow space between the cliff and the river is occupied by the town—tall houses with arches and balconies facing a quay of heavy masonry, beneath which runs the Segre, and whence there is one of those views which artists love, of a still reach of river, with an old mill, and delicate gradations of pink and blue-green distance. A long bridge of yellow stone is broken midway, and across the ruined piers a wooden causeway on huge beams leads to the old brown gateway of the town. Just at one of the most charming bends of this view is the Fonda San Luiz, a thoroughly Spanish hotel, but clean and comfortable, and possessing a delightful terrace overhanging the river.

LERIDA.

Through the driving fog, and up streets which were almost like cascades from the heavy rain which had fallen, we made our way to the old cathedral, which is now abandoned by the canons on account of the steepness of the ascent, but a visit to which Street declares to be alone worth all the journey from England. This visit is, however, difficult to accomplish, as, from its position inside the fortifications, a special order has to be obtained and countersigned by the governor and military authorities. The main edifice dates from 1230, and the cloisters are among the most beautiful in Europe, but cut up for barrack purposes. The fog prevented our seeing the grand view of the Pyrenees, but Lerida, the Roman Ilerda, lay stretched beneath, and the winding Segre, which is said to have proved fatal to the daughter of Herodias, who gallivanted upon its frozen waters till she fell through the ice, and it cut off her head, which continued to dance by itself.

Another hideous journey brought us to Manresa, where we arrived in the dark, and took a guide, to lead the way through the ankle-deep mud and up the steep, tortuous streets, quite impervious to carriages, to the Posada del Sol. The first aspect of our inn was not encouraging, when the boy who carried our bags opened a door into a stable, where a number of rough-looking men were drinking, and whence a filthy stair led to some bare brick-floored rooms, with pallet-beds and scanty furniture. As in all smaller posadas, looking-glasses are unknown here, so a small hand-glass may be conveniently carried. There was no washing-stand in our rooms, and when we remonstrated, a pie-dish was found for the ladies, but the landlady protested that for "los señores" such things were both unknown and unnecessary, as they could wash themselves at a public stone trough, of which there was one at the end of the passage, and another in the comedór (*salle à manger*); and at the latter, in fact, a Spanish traveller, in his shirt, coolly came to perform his ablutions while we were breakfasting. However, the willing kindness of our young hostess made up for much that was wanting; and a supper of broth, vegetables, and some rough scraps of boiled meat was supplied to us. In the evening we were amused by her *sang-froid* in receiving a visit from her lover in the room where we were, the one common room. When the time came for him to go, he looked round at us, and asked if he should kiss her as usual. "Certainly," she said; "why not?" Upon which he did kiss her — not once only.

But oh! how entirely Manresa itself makes up for any amount of suffering, when, having followed the filthy streets — not paved, but cut out of the living rock—for some distance, and having descended a rugged way between two walls, which looks as if it led to a stone quarry, the view from the esplanade before the church of St. Ignatius suddenly bursts upon your sight! In front rises the grand colegiata of El Seo, built of yellow-grey stone, perched on the summit of the dark rocks, broken into a thousand picturesque hollows, which are filled with little gardens, where Indian corn, and vines, and cypresses flourish. On the right rises range above range of gaily-painted houses of the most varied and irregular forms,—arches, balconies, overhanging galleries, little ledges of roof supporting tiny hanging gardens with ivy and jessamine tangling over their edge. Deep down in the abyss flows the Llobregat, crossed by its tall bridge of pointed arches, and ending at a richly carved stone cross on a high pedestal. Beyond the river are ranges of olive-clad hills, above which, as we were drawing in the afternoon, uprose in mid-air a glorious vision, lifted high into the sky: pinnacles, spires, turrets, sugar-loaves, pyramids of faint-grey rocks, so wonderful that it was almost impossible to believe them a reality and not a phantasmagoria—the mountains of Monserrat.

We seem to be following in the footsteps of Ignatius Loyola, who remained here, after his conversion, for a whole year in a cave, unknown by any, except his confessors. He fasted the whole week on water and bread (which he begged), and on Sunday indulged in a few boiled herbs strewn with ashes. He wore an iron girdle and a hair-shirt, scourged himself twice a day, slept little, and lay on the ground. Every day he spent seven hours on his knees in prayer, and he received the sacraments every Sunday. To mortify his former personal vanity, he went about begging with his face covered with dirt, his hair long and unkempt, and his beard and nails of appalling length. The children pelted him with stones. For a long time " he found no comfort in prayer, no relief in fasting, no remedy in disciplines, no consolation from the sacraments, and his soul was overwhelmed with bitter sadness. But eventually his tranquillity of mind was perfectly restored, and his soul overflowed with spiritual joy, and he afterwards assured F. Lainez that he had learned more of divine mysteries by prayer in one hour at Manresa, than all the doctors of the schools could ever have taught him."* He was consoled by the belief that the Virgin smiled constantly upon him from her sanctuary at Monserrat during the year of his penance.

The vast convent which contains the famous cave is jammed into the narrow space between the terrace and the precipice. Externally it is covered with sculpture, not in the best style, but very effective. Within, from the large church, a passage lined with pictures relating to the history of the Jesuits, leads to the "Santa Cueva," left in its rugged rock nature, only the lower part being incrusted with bas-reliefs, which can be examined by the light of the swinging lamps. On the altar is the crucifix of Loyola, from whose wounds blood is supposed to have streamed forth.

From the Cueva we mounted the opposite hill to El Seo, an interesting church, with a rich canopied entrance; within, dark and gloomy, with a small but effective coro, and some brilliant remains of the stained glass, of which the greater

* See Butler's "Lives of the Saints," vol. vii.

part was destroyed by the French. Here, at mass, the women all appear in white flannel hoods, and in the half light look like the dead in their shrouds, but the men wear mantas of the most gorgeous colours.

La Cueva and El Seo are the only two regular sights of Manresa, but inexhaustible is the ever-varying beauty of the views from the lovely walks on the heights above the Llobregat, in one of which, a stone cross, near the convent of Sta. Clara, marks a spot where Loyola used to preach.

The vision of Monserrat made us long for the nearer reality, but it was two days ere we could tear ourselves away from the beauties of Manresa. Then we took the train to Monistrol, which faces the great purple amphitheatre of mountains, and where, at the station, we found a *tartana* waiting— a round covered cart lined with carpet—in which we jolted up the hills for two hours and a half, the views becoming finer at every turn, till on a ledge of rock we suddenly came upon a tall cross, inscribed—"Aqùi se hizo la Santa Imagen en 880," and immediately found ourselves under the convent walls. A gateway, beside a wide-arched Gothic fountain, leads to the upper courts, on one side of which rise the conventual buildings themselves, with their half-ruined cloisters, and, on the other three, the immense suites of rooms destined for the reception of the pilgrims (of whom no less than 200,000 often come here in the month of September alone), and inscribed with the names of the different saints to whom they are dedicated—Santa Gertrudis, Santa Scholastica, Santa Teresa, San Alphonso, San Ignacio, &c.

We were assigned rooms in one of these: not uncomfortable, if their cold brick floors had had any fire-places to warm them. A man was sent to bring us some water, sheets, and towels, a little wood and charcoal was placed in the tiny kitchen which belonged to our apartment, and we were then left to shift for ourselves. Soon the bell warned us that the New Year's evening service was about to begin, and we hurried to the church, where, groping our way through the dark pillars, we took our seats close to the reja. There, so many candles were lighted around the altar, that the famous image—a black doll in a robe of silver tissue—shone forth resplendently. The priest who lighted the lamps, when he went up to her, kissed her on the cheeks. When all was ready a long procession of boys in surplices filed in and grouped themselves around the image. Then the strangest service began : singing, sweet and soft at first, but suddenly breaking off into the most discordant yells and shrieks, accompanied by a blowing of whistles and horns, beating of tin clappers, with fiddles, trumpets, and cymbals. There were about sixty performers, and a congregation of eight. Altogether it was most extraordinary, but we heard afterwards that this most unmelodious music was intended as typical of the rude worship of the shepherds at Bethlehem.

The image, like most of its kind, "black but comely," is attributed to St. Luke as a sculptor, and is said to have been brought to Barcelona by St. Peter in A.D. 30. During the Moorish invasion it lay hidden for sixty years in a cave, where its delicious scent discovered it to Bishop Gondemar, who attempted to remove it to Manresa, but when it reached an especial ledge of the mountain side it refused to move further. Hence an oratory arose on the spot, which was enlarged into a nunnery, converted in 976 into a Benedictine convent. The present church is due to Philip II., and was opened in 1599. It is of small interest. Some remnants of an earlier church, with the tomb of a young warrior, are preserved in the museum of the convent.

By lighting one match after another in the dark passages, we found our way back to our apartment, where we passed the night as the sole inhabitants of our vast wing of the convent. Only the hooting of an owl broke the silence, the bird which Spanish legend relates to have been present at the crucifixion, and ever since to have repeated in a terror and woe-stricken voice, "Cruz! cruz!"

Next morning we set off early up the mountains. It had frozen all night, and nothing could be lovelier than the effect of the thick hoar frost —every delicate leaf and blade of grass being encrusted with ice, and standing out like glistening diamonds against the grey fog. Without having seen a fog, no one should leave Monserrat, for, glorious as it is at all times, this natural veil lends an indescribable softness and mystery to the views, and the moment when the curtain draws up, and the sun bursts forth victoriously, is so intensely splendid. We were then in one of the high rock terraces, several miles above the convent, where no sound except the occasional cry of an eagle broke the entire stillness, for not a breath of air stirred the frost-laden boughs. Suddenly the mist rolled away, and in the distance was revealed on one side the long expanse of the

Mediterranean, from Barcelona to Tarragona, with the shining threads of rivers leading up to it through numberless towns and villages, and on the other the vast range of the Pyrenees, quite covered with snow, against the softest of blue skies. Deep below were the most tremendous abysses of rock, often perpendicular precipices of two and three thousand feet, but, wherever any soil could lodge, filled with the wealth of innumerable lovely shrubs—box, aliternus, laurestinus, filarœa, lentisck, euphorbia, and flowering heath,—all evergreens, which, according to the old Spanish tradition, are permitted to bear their leaves all the year round, because they sheltered the weariness of the Virgin Mother and the Holy Child during their flight into Egypt. Where these could not find foothold, the sides of the rock are clothed with cascades of honeysuckle, smilex, and jessamine. High in the rugged crags, remains of ruined hermitages seemed as if suspended over the face of the abyss, so utterly inaccessible that one would have thought the inmates could only have reached them by a miracle, and that it was quite impossible that the troops under Suchet should have climbed up thither to rob and murder when "they hunted the hermits like chamois along the cliffs."

The afternoon was occupied in visiting the different buildings of the convent and the relics they contain. Here again the chief historical interest comes from Ignatius Loyola, who came hither from Pamplona, as soon as he was cured of his wounds, and made a confession which lasted three days, to a saintly French monk who was then residing here. On his way up to the convent, he bought in the village a long coat of coarse cloth, a girdle, sandals, a wallet, and a pilgrim's staff. In the church he took a vow of perpetual chastity, and dedicated himself with the greatest fervour to the divine service. Then giving his horse to the monks, and hanging up his sword before the altar of the Virgin, in sign of renunciation of his temporal warfare, he walked away, barefoot and bareheaded, to his penance at Manresa.

On the second day of our stay we took provisions, and followed the winding paths, sometimes overhanging the perpendicular edge of the precipice, sometimes descending and burying themselves in deep ravines of box and ilex, till we reached the highest peak of the mountain group. Hence, the view is surpassingly magnificent. The whole of Catalonia, tossed and riven into myriad fantastic forms of hill and cleft, lies beneath, bounded only by the snowy ranges and the sea. So tremendous are the gorges into which you look down, that the eye can scarcely fathom their awful depths, and the birds descending into them, vanish away in the distance.

Just beneath the summit is the ruined hermitage of S. Geronimo, the furthest, but one of the easiest of access, of the many now desolated retreats which were so eagerly sought after by the devotional feeling of the Middle Ages, and where many of the proudest and noblest Spaniards passed their latter years in absolute solitude, attending to their own humble wants, and in a life of constant penance and prayer. Two little rooms remain here, with the paved terrace and the stone seat of the hermit, and certainly it would be hard for him to find a more heaven-inspiring place than this silent mountain peak, looking down through all the glories of nature upon the world he had renounced.

The ascent to S. Geronimo occupies about three hours, but we were away nine hours altogether. As we were returning, just as the bell of the convent, from its green invisible depths, gave notice, amid mountain echoes, of the Ave

Maria, an enchanter's wand seemed to smite the heavens, which above the sea burst into a crimson flush, melting into the most delicate emerald, while every crag of the valley glowed as if tipped with burnished gold, rising from its purple chasms; and then, silently, the blue veil arose and shrouded peak after peak, gorgeous in colour at first, but solemnly fading till all Nature was asleep beneath a grey mantle.

On the third day we set of in quite another direction, taking a precipitous path which winds around the gorge beneath the convent to the Cave of the Virgin, where the famous image was concealed during the Moorish occupation, angels guiding the priests who bore it, over rift and chasm, to a place of safety. We had taken the key from the convent, which admitted us to the cave, now a chapel, perched eyrie-like on the edge of the ravine, where a series of bas-reliefs tell the story of the shrine, and behind which a convent contains a pretty Gothic cloister with a well. Another path afterwards led us to the Cueva de Garin, where a painted stone figure commemorates a hermit, who long lived there on his hands and knees, and where his basket, pitcher, &c., are preserved. Behind the convent, a narrow strip of flat ground is occupied by a garden full of roses,—roses, which were white once, say the monks, and which owe their present purple colour to a drop of the Saviour's blood, which fell upon their leaves from the cross, as they bloomed on Mount Calvary. These are only a few out of a thousand subjects for the pencil, each more enchanting than the last; the enormous pinnacles of rock, the rugged pathways with their stone crosses and hermitages, and the ancient evergreen shrubs, combining at every step into fresh and better composition with the delicate pinks and blues of the mountain distance. Monserrat besides has the advantage of being a most comfortable place to stay at, as, though only lodging is given by the monks (for a voluntary payment, none is asked), there is an excellent Fonda in the courtyard of the convent, which provides as good food as can be found it Barcelona itself. The air is the purest and most reviving imaginable, and even in the first days of January the cold was not greater than in the valleys, as the monastery is so sheltered, while the rich growth of aloes attests the dryness of the soil; and on the higher terraces, in the brilliant sunshine, it was almost too hot. Altogether it is wonderful that Monserrat, surely far more beautiful than any single spot in France, Switzerland, Germany, or Italy, and so easily accessible in two days from the south of France (*via* Gerona and Barcelona), should be almost unknown to English tourists.

III.

BARCELONA AND GERONA.

Fonda del Oriente, Barcelona, *January* 14, 1872.

THE life and animation of Barcelona are charming. As we drove into the town, after leaving the solitudes of Monserrat, it seemed as if the whole of the gay, pleasure-loving population must be in the streets. So crowded were they with people on foot, that a carriage could scarcely pass. The shops, brilliantly lighted, were full of dolls innumerable; for it was the eve of the Befana—every possible phase of dollhood finding its representative, from old men and women down to babies in cradles. The children themselves were rushing about, blowing tin trumpets and whistles, and beating little drums; organs were grinding, guitars were twanging, fans were flashing through the soft air in the fingers of dark-veiled señoras, and over all extended a cloudless, deep-blue heaven, fretted with brilliant stars.

BARCELONA.

Through the centre of the town runs for nearly a mile the beautiful Rambla, formed by an avenue of arching plane-trees, enclosing a broad walk for foot-passengers, while the carriage-ways are on either side. The Rambla is the centre and axis of life in Barcelona. Here are all the principal hotels, and hence all the best streets diverge. The lower division is the fashionable walk of the aristocracy, and is full of smart people, but at the upper extremity, where the peasants chiefly congregate, is the bird and flower market, where multitudes of canaries are sold daily amid the great bunches of heliotrope, and where the most wonderful mantas are to be seen, of scarlet, blue, and gold, flowing from the shoulders of rough-looking men, who would be content with the common dress of ploughmen in England. At the lower end of the Rambla begins the Muralla del Mar, a delightful terrace, sheltered and sunny, overhanging the port and shipping, though raised high above them, and with views across the still reaches of water to the fortified hill of Montjuich, which rises abruptly from the sea, like Shakespeare's cliff at Dover. To ascend this hill towards sunset is quite a duty with visitors to Barcelona, for from thence, across a foreground of wild aloes, which are here frequently formed into hedges, the whole white town is seen like a map, lying in its brown, burnt-up plain, surrounded by mountains, the flat tops of the houses giving it a peculiarly eastern appearance, for there are no sloping roofs in Barcelona.

The streets in the heart of the town are thoroughly dull and unpicturesque; and it is after following one of the dingiest of all, bounded by high, drab-coloured walls, that suddenly a wide gothic arch admits one into a vast, arcaded quadrangle, perfectly bathed in light and sunshine. Here huge orange-trees, whose boughs are weighed almost to the ground by their massive bunches of golden fruit, rise amid plantations of tree-like geraniums, and fountains splash gaily in the sunbeams.. It is not like one's ideal of a cathedral cloister, yet such it is, and wonderfully interesting is it to watch the ever-varying representations of life here—the solemn canons, with their breviaries, pacing up and down, and toiling through their appointed task of psalm-saying; the polite old beggars, the men in their bright mantas and scarlet barrettas, the women in their blue petticoats and white handkerchiefs over their heads; the children, who shout, and feed the canons' geese with bread—for on the largest of the fountains live the famous geese which have been kept here from time immemorial to guard the treasures of the cathedral, according to the old Catalonian custom, which makes geese serve, and more efficaciously too, the place of watch-dogs at the country houses. In the centre of the Fontana de las Ocas is a little bronze figure of a knight on a horse, which spouts water from its nostrils, while its tail is indicated by a long jet of silvery spray. This is not St. George, but the brave knight Vilardell, full of good works, who was permitted to kill the famous dragon, but who forgot his humility in the moment of triumph, and exclaimed, "Well done, good sword! Well done, brave arm of Vilardell!" upon which a drop of the dragon's poisonous blood fell upon his arm from the sword which he brandished, and he died. This is the first moral inculcated upon the childish mind of Barcelona, which is intimately familiar with Vilardell, who is again represented, in his combat with the dragon, over an archway in the street leading to the cathedral.

A grand round-headed arch leads from the cloister into the church, begun in 1298, but chiefly built, from designs by Jaques Fabra, in the beginning of the fourteenth century. It is beautiful and solemn beyond description, only faintly lighted by the rich stained windows at either end, whose coloured lights are almost lost amid the many chapels and tall reed-like pillars. Beneath the altar lies Santa Eulalia, the "well-speaking" virgin, martyred by Dacian in 309, and transferred hither in 878 from Santa Maria del Mar, where she was previously buried, two kings, three queens, and four princesses attending, since which time all Spanish sovereigns, down to Christina and Isabella, have been wont to pass the night in prayer before her shrine. There is another saint here also, Oldagar, invoked in childbirth, who died 1137, and was discovered five hundred years after "quite uncorrupted, except the tip of his nose." His sleeping effigy is raised aloft over the altar of the first chapel on the right of the nave. From beneath the organ hangs a hideous Saracen's head, with gaping mouth, starting eyes, and a vast flowing beard. Such, it is said, were found useful in animating the crusaders. A great deal is written in the various English guidebooks about the peculiar lighting of this cathedral by windows pierced through from the chapels of the nave to the chapels back to back with them, which open upon the cloisters; but if such arrangement ever existed, there is certainly no trace of it now.

Many of the other churches are worth visiting, and are interesting specimens of the peculiar types of architecture to which they belong: San Pablo del Campo and San Pedro de las Puellas, of the very earliest Catalonian, with heavy, low, round-headed arches; Santa Maria del Mar, built 1328—1483, a grand single nave of remarkable simplicity, with enormous octagonal columns; and, most especially, the Colegiata of Santa Ana, of 1146, with a lovely silent Gothic cloister, filled with grand old orange-trees, more beautiful even than those of the cathedral. Here authorised and highly respectable old beggars sit all day long upon chairs, on the chance of a stray cuarto.

"Pardon me, my sister; does not your worship see that I am drawing?" I said to one of them, who had hobbled away from her throne to beg.

"Ah Dios!" she answered. "Blind that I was! worm that I am! so your worship draws. And I —I too am a lover of the arts."

And ever after we were the best of friends, and as I came to the cloister in the morning I received the friendliest of nods from my art-loving sister, who never dreamt of begging again.

The remains of domestic architecture are scarcely less interesting than the churches, and many of the older houses retain their graceful patios, with cloistered external staircases, covered with arabesques. In the Casa Consistorial is a fine Gothic hall, in which ancient councils were held; but the gem is the Casa de la Disputacion, where a beautiful external stair leads to the rich chapel of St. George, and a lovely Gothic court, full of orange-trees and flowers. The old palace which contains the archives of the kings of Arragon is also well worth visiting. The Archivio is reached by a staircase, adorned with a statue of Vilardell, and with a fine Moorish ceiling, and contains many thousand splendid manuscript volumes and illuminated missals from suppressed convents, all arranged on low stands, that they may be kept constantly dusted and free from worms,—an arrangement rather to the detriment of their effect as a library.

The climate of Barcelona is delightful. During the ten days of early January which we passed there, we never once experienced the slightest sensation of cold; fires were unthought of, and we sate with windows wide open at eight o'clock in the morning. Quite into the middle of the night the Rambla was filled with gay crowds; ladies enjoying the starlight in their transparent mantillas, without veils or shawls. The sturdy growth of the lemons, which perish in three degrees of frost, is an evidence of the warmth; as well as the profusion of delicate Australian gum-trees, and the masses of heliotrope still in bloom. This eastern vegetation is greatly assisted by the dryness of the temperature, only sixty-five days on the average being wet in the whole year; so that Barcelona is an admirable winter residence for invalids.

Many pleasant excursions may be made from hence, especially that to the grand ruined abbey of Ripoll, and to San Culgat del Vallis near Serdanola. From the end of the Rambla, a miniature railway carries passengers in a few minutes to Sarria, a village at the foot of the hills, famous for its pepper-trees, which here attain the most enormous size. Hence a deep lane, overhung with huge aloes, leads in half an hour to the desolated monastery of Pedralles, with its graceful tower and fine stained glass. The hillside here is occupied by many villas of rich Barcelonese merchants; but these by no means interfere with the wild grace of the view, especially charming at sunset, when behind the dark monastery, with its solemn tower and cypresses, Barcelona is seen glowing in the golden haze, backed by the deep-blue sea.

Nothing can be more charming than the environs of Barcelona in winter, which may be most pleasantly spent in a villa near Sarria, but in summer the sun beats pitilessly upon its sandy hillsides, and the ground is cracked into a thousand widely opening rifts by its power. Lizards abound here and rejoice in the sunshine, and the dangerous tarantula is not unfrequently met with. Spanish legend tells us that the tarantula was once a foolish and impudent woman who had such a passion for dancing, that she never ceased to dance even when the Divine Master was passing by, but conducted herself with appalling irreverence. Therefore the Saviour rebuked her by converting her into a spider, with a guitar stamped upon its back, and ordained that its bite should cause all those bitten by it to dance, till they fell down fainting and exhausted. Most picturesque is all such Spanish folk-lore, and in no country is it more abundant. Of the serpent it tells, that, after its triumph in the Garden of Eden, it always went erect and swollen with pride, till it met with the Holy Family during their flight into Egypt, and audaciously attempted to bite the Infant Jesus: then St. Joseph indignantly rebuking it, bade it lie down and never rise up again, and ever since it has crawled on the ground.

No one should leave Barcelona without visiting the street of the Plateria, entirely lined with jewellers' shops, filled with ornaments which retain the antique patterns derived from the Moors, or from old Greek designs. The heavy *joyas*, set with amethysts and emeralds, are especially remarkable. There is a small English church at Barcelona—an upper chamber, in a central situation, prettily fitted up.

We had always regretted having been prevented entering Spain from Toulouse, as we should then have seen Perpignan, so remarkable as exhibiting a transitional town, semi-Spanish, semi-French; and St. Elne, which is a most curious link between the early mediæval Spanish and the early mediæval French buildings. On this route we should also have naturally visited Gerona, to which we determined to retrace our steps from Barcelona.

Four hours of railroad, by the inland line which passes the quaint old town of Hostalrich, gave us the strange experience of leaving sunshine and warmth and blooming heliotrope, and within two hours finding ourselves amidst hoar-frost and ice and a nipped, frozen vegetation. At Gerona, however, the sun had conquered winter, and the old town, under the protection of its fortified hill, gleamed forth with its white balconied houses, topped by the cathedral. We walked from the station to the Fonda España (once Estrella), in itself an interesting house, with beautiful *ajimcz* windows—*i.e.* Gothic windows—divided by slender, round pillars, generally of marble; the Arabic name meaning "windows by which the sun enters." The cathedral, reached by a lofty flight of steps, is not interesting outside; but within, the immense width of its nave gives it a certain grandeur, and is of a size which one scarcely realises, except by comparing the dimensions of this church of a fifth-rate Spanish town with those of our finest English cathedrals; the width of Gerona being seventy-three feet, of Canterbury forty-three, York fifty-two, Westminster thirty-eight. The retablo is of silver,—the cloisters, on low but richly-carved Byzantine pillars, are well worth examination; also the Puerta de los Apostolos, with the statues of the saints all standing inside a porch of immense width. Behind the cathedral a rugged path winds up the hillside beneath the fortifications, and gives perhaps the best view which can be obtained of the town and its towers standing out against the bright green vega, and delicate distance of pink mountains.

Two other churches should be visited—S. Pedro de los Gallegans, a grand specimen of tenth-century Romanesque,—and S. Feliu (Felix), with a beautiful truncated spire, dedicated to the missionary of Augsburg, and remarkable as containing the image of S. Narcissus, a patriotic doll, which, when its country was menaced with invasion, had the power of immediately becoming purulent, and producing innumerable legions of flies, of so poisonous a nature, that in 1285 they stung to death 40,000 Frenchmen and 24,000 horses, and, as late as 1684, demolished an entire French army; prodigies which not unnaturally led the local junta to declare S. Feliu their captain-general in 1808, and to lay the staff of command upon his shrine!

IV.

TARRAGONA AND POBLET.

Fonda de Europa, Tarragona, *January* 24.

BETWEEN Barcelona and Tarragona we stayed for a few hours at Martorell to sketch the famous bridge, which strides across the gulf of the Llobregat, between the barest, most arid rocks imaginable. The original bridge dates from 535 A.U.C., when it was erected by Hannibal in honour of Hamilcar, and the triumphal gate at its entrance is of this date; but the high pointed arch of the bridge itself is due to the Moors. It is generally called "El Puerta del Diablo," like so many other curious steep old bridges, ascribed to the Devil, in almost every country of Europe. Hence, once more, we looked upon the glorious peaks of Monserrat.

Tarragona is disappointing. So much has been said about it lately, and so much that does not contain a particle of truth; for instance, a recent agreeable writer describes the wanderer on its ramparts as looking down upon a green plain, studded with noble palms,—whereas the practical mind sees nothing but a stony wilderness, in which not the vestige of a tree, much less of a palm-tree, can be found. The so-called Rambla is a dingy, drab avenue of poor whitewashed houses, between which some meagre plane-trees seem vainly struggling into existence, and where the wretched population, promenading in rags, follow you to beg, even up the staircase of your hotel. Yet even Tarragona can offer much compensation for its evil smells, evil meats, and mendicant neighbours. The cathedral, built 1089 to 1131, is magnificent. The west front rises above a steep flight of steps at the end of the principal street, and, though unfinished, has a grand rose window, and a portal surrounded by statues of saints, and some empty niches, to account for which it is said that one of these holy ones, wearied with his stiff position, comes down from his pedestal every hundred years, and goes his way. Within, all is gloriously in keeping, the grand Romanesque arches being uninjured by paint or whitewash, and their gloom relieved by the lower walls being hung with faded tapestries, exceedingly effective, bought in London at the sale of church furniture by Henry VIII., and said to have once decorated St. Paul's. Santa Tecla, the tutelar of Tarragona, who heads the peerage of virgin martyrs, has a fine marble chapel. But here, as in so many Spanish churches, the gem of all is the cloister, —a noble arcaded court of varied, round-headed arches, enclosing a most lovely garden, full of summer beauty and sunshine, even in January.

We have walked from Tarragona to the so-called tomb of the Scipios, about three miles distant on the sea-coast. It is a desolate, massive Roman tomb, like many of those on the Appian way, with two mouldering figures discernible on its front, and is well situated in a fragment of ancient forest pines, with an undergrowth of palmito, or dwarf shrubby palm—quite an oasis in this arid, stormy country. Another day we followed the Lerida road for two miles, to a wild, rocky valley, full of palmito, which is crossed by a grand Roman aqueduct with a double tier of arches. The town itself abounds in Roman fragments, and some huge stones are shown as part of the palace of Augustus, who passed the winter here in 26 B.C. But, in spite of these attractions,

CATHEDRAL, TARRAGONA

travellers, especially invalids, should beware of trusting to the guide-book recommendations of Tarragona, especially that of Murray, who says— "As a winter residence for invalids few places in Europe can equal this, whilst the walks are excellent and varied, and the carriage-drives numerous, leading in various directions through shady pine-woods and oak plantations," &c. The fact being that the situation of the town, high above the sea, on an isolated hill, is exceedingly exposed; that there are three drives, but no decent carriage wherewith to take them; and that the pine-woods are a fiction, while, as for oaks, there is not one in the country.

The most interesting thing to be attained here is the excursion to Poblet, which no Spanish travellers should on any account be induced to omit.

We took our tickets in the dark, by the 6.20 train, to Montblanch, on the Lerida line, passing on the way Reus, the birthplace of Prim, where the sword of his African campaigns is preserved as a precious relic in the town-hall. At eight we reached Montblanch, and from the crowd of ragged people at the station, disentangled a man who said that he had a tartana at our service, and followed him to it through the deep mire of the wretched streets. It was the humblest of vehicles —a rude round framework of unplaned open bars, nailed one to the other, and covered with carpet; and with no bottom but ropes knotted together. A headstrong mule was found, which with difficulty could be induced to move, but which, when once it set off, put its head up in the air, and galloped straight forward, regardless of obstacles, sending us violently from side to side of the tartana, as it pitched and jerked over a road which alternated between bare rock and deep sloughs of mud. In vain did the driver beseech us to sit forward; we had no sooner climbed to the front, and seized tight hold of its bars, than a tremendous lurch sent us all rolling backward, with our feet twisted through the open ropes beneath. The driver, however, never ceased to shriek, yelp, and scold at the mule; and though the road grew worse at every bound we made, we got along somehow—till, when the towers of Poblet were rising in view, we could bear it no longer, and, begging to be let out, found we advanced much more quickly on foot.

The sun was just breaking through the clouds, which had obscured the earlier morning, and lit up the lonely hollow of the hills in which the convent is situated. Venerable olive trees, their trunks gnarled and twisted into myriad strange forms, lined the rugged, rock-hewn way; and behind them stretched ranges of hills; here, rich and glowing with woody vegetation where the sun caught their projecting buttresses,—there, lost in the purple mists of their deep rifts. The approach to a great religious house was indicated, first by a tall stone cross rising on a lofty pedestal, stained with golden lichen and with myrtle and lentisck growing in the hollows of its grey stones; then by a strange group of saintly figures in stone, standing aloft amid a solitary grove of pillars at a crossway, and marking, as we were afterwards told, the afternoon walk of the friars. Hence an avenue, with broken stone seats at intervals on either side, leads up to the convent walls,—a clear, sparkling mountain torrent singing by its side, in a basin overhung with fern and tall water-plants. Then, after skirting the walls for some distance, an ancient gateway admits one to the interior of what, till within a few years ago, was the largest religious house, and one of the largest buildings in Europe.

No remains elsewhere impress the beholder

with the same sense of melancholy as the convent of Poblet. An English ruin, softened and mellowed by time, fading and crumbling by a gentle, gradual decay, can give no idea of it. Here, it is the very abomination of desolation. It is all fresh; it might be all perfect now, but it is the most utterly ruined ruin that can exist. Violence and vengeance are written on every stone. The vast walls, the mighty courts, the endless cloisters, look as if the shock of a terrible earthquake had passed over them. There is no soothing vegetation, no ivy, no flowers, and the very intense beauty and delicacy of the fragments of sculpture which remain in the riven and rifted walls, where they were too high up for the spoiler's hand to reach them, only make stronger contrast with the coarse gaps where the outer coverings of the walls have been violently torn away, and where the marble pillars and beautiful tracery lie dashed to atoms upon the ground.

The convent was founded in 1149 by Ramon Berenguer IV., on the spot where mystic lights had revealed the body of Poblet, a holy hermit, who had taken refuge here during the Moorish occupation. Every succeeding monarch increased its wealth, regarding it, not only in the light of a famous religious shrine, but as his own future resting-place; for hither, over moor and mountain, all the earlier kings of Arragon were brought to be buried. As the long lines of royal tombs rose thicker on either side of the choir, the living monarchs came hither too, for a retreat of penitence and prayer, and lived for a time the conventual life. And thus, though no sovereign ever actually assumed the cowl at Poblet, several left orders that their effigy should be twice represented on their monuments, once in royal robes, and again in the monastic habit. Five hundred monks of St. Bernard occupied, but did not fill, the magnificent buildings; their domains became almost boundless, their jewelled chalices and gorgeous church furniture could not be reckoned. The library of Poblet became the most famous in Spain, so that it was said that a set of waggons employed for a whole year could not cart away the books. As Poblet became the Westminster Abbey of Spain as regarded its kings and queens, so it gradually also answered to Westminster in becoming the resting-place of all other eminent persons, who were brought hither to mingle theirs with the royal dust. Dukes and grandees of the first class occupied each his niche around the principal cloister, where their tombs, less injured than anything else, form a most curious and almost perfect epitome of the history of Spanish sepulchral decoration. Marquises and counts, less honoured, had a cemetery assigned them in the strip of ground surrounding the apse; famous warriors were buried in the nave and ante-chapel; and the bishops of Lerida and Tarragona, deserting their own cathedrals, had each their appointed portion of the transept; while the abbots of Poblet, far mightier than bishops, occupied the chapter-house, where numbers of their venerable effigies, typical of dignity and repose, may still be seen, having been hastily covered over at the time of the invasion. Gradually the monks of Poblet became more exclusive; their number was reduced to sixty-six, but into that sacred circle no novice was introduced in whose veins ran other than the purest blood of a Spanish grandee. He who became a monk of Poblet had to prove his pedigree, and the chapter sate in solemn deliberation upon his quarterings. Every monk had his two servants, and rode upon a snow-white mule. The mules of the friars were sought through the whole peninsula at an enormous expense. Within the walls, every variety of trade was represented; no monk need seek for anything beyond his cloister; the tailors, the shoemakers, the apothecaries, had each their wing or court. Hospitals were raised on one side for sick and ailing pilgrims: on the other rose a palace appropriated to the sovereigns who sought the cure of their souls. The vast produce of the vineyards of the mountainous region which depended upon Poblet, was brought to the great convent wine-presses, and was stowed away in its avenue of wine-vats. "El Priorato" became one of the most reputed wines in the country; the pipes, the presses, and the vats where it was originally prepared, still remain almost entire.

Year by year the power of the convent increased, till, like autocratic sovereigns, the friars of Poblet issued their commands, and the surrounding country had only to hear and obey. He who failed to attend to the summons of their mass-bell, had to answer to the monks for his neglect. Strange rumours began to float of peasants who, entering the convent gates, had never been known to come forth. Gradually the monks became the bugbear of neighbouring children, and threats, which tampered with their names, were whispered by the lace-making mothers in the ears of their naughty little ones. At last came the wars of

Don Carlos. Then political dissensions arose within the mystic circle; half the monks were royalists, half were Carlists, and the latter considering themselves oppressed, and muttering vengeance, whispered abroad tales of secret dungeons and of hidden torture. The public curiosity became excited. Many yet live who remember the scene when the convent doors were broken in by night, and the townsfolk, streaming through court and cloister, reached the room which had been designated, where, against a wall, by which it may still be traced, the dreaded rack was found, and beneath it a dungeon filled with human bones, and with other instruments of torture. Twenty-four hours were insisted upon by the authorities to give the friars a chance of safety: they escaped, but only with their lives. Poblet, beautiful Poblet, was left in all its riches and perfection; nothing was taken away.

Then the avenging torrents streamed up the mountain side and through the open portals. All gave way before them; nothing was spared. "Destroy, destroy!" was the universal outcry. Every weapon of destruction was pressed into service. No fatigue, no labour was evaded. Picture, and shrine, and tomb, and fresco, fell alike under the destroying hammer; till, wearied with devastation, the frantic mob could work no more, and fire was set to the glorious sacristy, while the inestimable manuscripts of the library, piled heap upon heap, were consumed to ashes.

At the present time the story of that day of destruction is engraved on every wall. At first, you are unprepared. The little decorated chapel of St. George, on the right of the second entrance, is so little injured, that it might be taken for an ordinary ruin; then, passing the gate, one finds the remains of a series of frescoes, which tell the story of the Moorish invasion. Only the figure of one warrior and of the avenging angel are left, the rest is torn away; the lower pillars are gone, but their beautiful capitals, of monks seated amid rich foliage, are left.

Hence one reaches the original front of the convent. On the left is another chapel, windowless and grass-grown, and behind it the remains of the hospital, which is reduced to a mere shell. In front, rise on one side the heavy machicolated towers which once flanked the main entrance, now bricked up,—and on the other, between statues of San Bernardo and San Benito, the entrance of the church. Here, in the ante-chapel, donkeys have their stalls around the tombs of kings, and the fragments of the royal monuments lie piled one upon another. On the right, in a dark niche, is the Easter Sepulchre, richly wrought in marble: only the figure of the Saviour has been spared; the Virgin and saints, legless, armless, and noseless, stand weeping around. Below, a sleeping archbishop has escaped with less injury.

The Coro retains its portals of lumachella marble, but within it is utterly desolate, though overhead the grand vaulting of the roof, and its supporting columns, are perfectly entire. There is no partition now beyond this, and through the pillared avenue the eye pierces to the high altar, where the splendid retablo of white marble still stands erect, though all its delicate reliefs are shattered to fragments, even the figure of the infant Saviour being torn from the arms of the central Madonna. Here, perhaps, is the climax of the destruction. On either side were the royal tombs; Jaime El Conquistador; Alonzo II.; Ferdinand I. and his two sons, Juan II. and Alonzo V.; Pedro IV. and his three queens; Juan I. and his two, with many princes and princesses of royal blood. The monuments remain, but so altered, so battered with chisel and hammer, that scarcely a fragment of their beautiful ornaments is intact, and the effigies have entirely disappeared. Caryatides without arms or faces, floating angels wingless and headless, flowers without stems, and leaves without branches, all dust-laden, cracked, and crumbling, scarcely testify to what they have been; and thus it is throughout. From the sacristy blackened with fire, where one portion of the gorgeous Venetian framework still hangs in mockery, one is led to the dormitory of the novices, where the divisions of the cells may be traced, though none are left, and to the refectory, in which the fountain may still be seen, where, in this hot climate, the luxury of iced water always played during dinner in a central marble bason, while, from a stone pulpit, a reader refreshed the souls of the banqueters. The great cloister remains comparatively entire, surrounded with tombs, and enclosing, amid a thicket of roses which have survived the fate of all else, a portico, with a now dry fountain, once of many streams, where the monks in summer afternoons were wont to be regaled with chocolate. This was voluntary chocolate; but another room is shown in which is remembered that obligatory chocolate was served every morning, for fear any brother should faint during the celebration of mass. Beyond the great cloister, which is of the richest pointed architecture,—every capital varied in fresh varieties of sculpture,—is an earlier cloister, formed by low, narrow, round-headed, thick-set arches of the twelfth century. Above one side of the great cloister, rich in the delicate tracery of its still remaining widows, rises the shell of the palace of Martino El Humilde. Space would not suffice to describe in detail each court with its distinctive features, through which the visitor is led in increasing wonder and distress, to the terrible torture-chamber, which is wisely shown last, as offering the clue and key to the whole. But surely no picture that the world can offer of the sudden destruction of human power can be more appalling than fallen Poblet, beautiful still, but most awful, in the agony of its unexpected destruction!

In the summer, the solitude is broken by a perfect school of young architects, from Italy, Prussia, and America, who come hither to study; but in England Poblet is little known. The time is so short since its destruction, that of the sixty-six monks who occupied the convent at the time, many are still living. At Poblet they wore the white Bernardine habit, and at mass they officiated in long trains of white; but the feeling against them is still so bitter, that if one of them reappeared in his former costume he would be immediately assassinated. Each has retired to his family. We asked the guide if none had ever revisited their former home. "Yes," he said, "five of the friars came last summer; but they could not bear to look. They wept and sobbed the whole time they were here; it was piteous to see them." From the ruins of their old home must have come back to them with thrilling force, an echo from the hymn of their Founder so often chaunted within its walls :—

>"Hortus odoribus affluet omnibus, hic paradisus,
> Plenaque gratia, plenaque gaudia, cantica, risus;
> Plena redemptio, plena refectio, gloria plena :
> Vi, lue, luctibus aufugientibus, exule pœnâ.
> Nil ibi debile, nil ibi flebile, nil ibi scissum;
> Res ibi publica pax erit unica, pax in idipsum.
> Hic furor, hic mala, schismata, scandala, pax sine pace;
> Pax sine litibus, et sine luctibus in Syon arce."

V.

VALENCIA, ALICANTE, AND ELCHE.

Hotel Peregrino, Murcia, *February* 2.

WE travelled all night from Tarragona to Valencia, a most fatiguing journey of eleven hours, in a train which rattled and shook beyond description, making sleep quite impossible. We were obliged to console ourselves with the conversation of our fellow-travellers, and many are the pleasant glimpses into the national life and character one may gain at such times. One woman remarked to another how sweetly her baby was smiling in its sleep. "Yes," she said, "it is laughing at the angels, which it only can see." "I have such a buzzing in my ears," said an old woman to another. "It is the sound of a leaf," she answered, "falling from the Tree of Life."

Day broke in time to show us the first vision of tall palms, with their feathery foliage rising black against one of Tennyson's "daffodil skies," which above, still deep blue, was filled with stars. A truly southern mob greeted our arrival, shrieking out the merits of the opposition hotels, and trying to appropriate us and our packages by force. Woe betide the traveller who on such occasions has not chosen his resting-place; but its name had made us already decide upon the Fonda del Cid, which well deserves recommendation, and was, in fact, the first thoroughly comfortable hotel we had met with in Spain. Opposite the windows rises the tall semi-Moorish tower of the Miguelete, built by Juan Franck, 1381—1418, which, with the magnificent gate called Puerta de Serranos (1349), and the Gothic Lonja, or town-hall (1482), are almost the only ancient buildings of importance which remain in Valencia, where, unlike other Spanish towns, a perfect warfare against the antiquities has been carried on for some years past, the ajimez windows having been almost all modernised, and the whole of the grand old walls having been pulled down after King Amadeo's visit in 1871, "in order to give employment to the poor" (!), though the condition of the streets is disgraceful, and the roads are left in such a state of neglect as to be utterly impassable; the principal one, leading to

El Grao, the port of Valencia, being like a ploughed field, with the furrows a yard deep. For some unaccountable reason the avenue of fine old trees which lined this road, was demolished at at the same time as the walls. The most interesting historical fragment in the town was pulled down by its idiotic authorities in 1865, and its site is now only marked by an inscription on a wall. This was the tower Albufat, upon which the cross was first hoisted when the Cid took Valencia from the Moors, after a twenty years' siege, in 1094, with the famous gate adjoining, the Puerta del Cid, by which he entered the town. From hence, in the moment of triumph, he sent back a command that the enemy should be permitted to bury their dead, and when the Moorish chieftain, touched by the unexpected clemency, sent two beautiful slaves for his acceptance, replied that to him, for whom the welcome of his own Ximena was waiting, no other charms could offer any attraction. Here, his first act was to take Ximena with her daughters, Sol and Elvira, to the top of the tower, and bid them look down upon the glories of the Huerta, the garden of Spain, which his perseverance at length had conquered. Here, in 1099, he lay upon his death-bed, surrounded by all his beloved ones, even his famous war-steed, Bavieca, being brought into the chamber, and "standing there like a lamb" to gaze upon his dying master. From this gate also once more the Cid rode forth upon Bavieca, upright in death, his corpse arrayed in full armour, with the face uncovered and his white beard falling down over his breastplate, supported by Gil Diaz and the Bishop Geronimo, and followed by the faithful Ximena and his warriors; a sight so awful that the Moors—who, regaining courage at the news of his death, had again encamped against the town—fled in terror, leaving the strange funeral procession to carry out the chieftain's last wish that he should be laid in S. Pedro de Cerdeña, and abandoning so great a booty to the Christians that, in the words of the old ballad, the Cid, even after death, won such riches from the heathen that "the poorest became rich."

No breath from these heroic days now blows upon Valencia, which is a very concentration of dulness, stagnation, and ugliness; its cathedral, chiefly Corinthian, is poor and featureless; none of the churches are fine; the dusty gardens of Alameda and Glorieta are ill-kept and rubbishy, and the handsome bridges, even in January, cross only a dry bed, without the smallest streamlet of water. In the market many picturesque costumes, however, may be seen and admired; swarthy labourers of the Huerta, with sandals, linen drawers, velvet jackets, flowing mantas of scarlet and blue, and their heads bound tight with a gaily-covered handkerchief, knotted behind, with the ends hanging down; women of the lower classes, in bright handkerchiefs also over their black hair, and of the upper classes, invariably in the mantilla, which is so much the rule here, that English ladies who do not wear them are followed, much as an Indian in feathers would be in Regent Street, and those of our party who went to see Ribera's pictures at the Colegio Patriarca, were forcibly ejected from the church for venturing to enter it in bonnets.

We stayed till Friday afternoon, in order to be present at the morning ceremonies of that day in the chapel of Corpus Christi in this college. At ten A.M. the congregation, all in black, take their places near the high-altar, which on ordinary occasions is surmounted by a Last Supper of Ribera; around this many tapers are burning, but the rest of the naturally gloomy church is additionally darkened. In front of the altar the priests kneel in silence, while the penitential psalms are sung by a hidden choir. Then, as the *Miserere* swells in thrilling notes through the gloom, the picture over the altar descends by an invisible machinery, and violet curtains are seen within. Gradually, as the chant proceeds, one veil after another is withdrawn; lilac, grey, black, till, when the imagination is fully aroused, appears, deeply recessed and dimly shewn by a quivering torchlight, the figure of the dying Saviour upon the Cross, only the bent head fully lighted up into a vividness of reality; the rest of the figure rather expressed than seen. The whole service is most impressive and touching, and can scarcely be witnessed without emotion. The last veil is only drawn for a few minutes, and as it is closed again, and the people rise from their knees, the joyful notes of the organ, accompanied by a chorus of voices, tell of the Resurrection and a new life.

The painters of Valencia form a separate school of their own, and are largely represented in their native town. The most remarkable were Juanes (1523—1597), who answers in Spain to Raphael; Francisco di Ribalta (1551—1628), who is compared with Domenichino; Josef Ribera or Spagnuoletto (1588—1666); Espinoza (1600—1680); and Orrente

(1560—1644), who is chiefly remarkable as a painter of cattle. The confiscated convent of El Carmen is now the Museo, and contains, amid a vast amount of trash, some pictures of Ribera and Ribalta, powerful, but chiefly of the black-agony school, excruciating representations of ecstasies, St. Francis, Santa Teresa, &c. One specimen of Ribalta, however, rises far above the rest, "The Nailing to the Cross," in which the Saviour, seated upon the slightly-inclined cross, on which He is being fastened, looks up to heaven in rapt contemplation, while one of the thieves, standing near, with his hands bound, watches with intense interest the preparations of the cross to which He is to be fixed. In striking contrast to these subjects, dark both in conception and execution, are some lovely works of Juanes, especially the Saviour instituting the Sacrament of the Lord's Supper, which is quite sublime in its touching solemnity of expression, and the picture called "La Purisima," painted, after long fasting and prayer, to represent the Virgin as she was described by the Jesuit, Martino de Alvaro, as having appeared to him in a vision. Still more beautiful works of Juanes may be seen over two altars in the Church of St. Nicolas, which contains a perfect gallery of this flower of Spanish painters, its masterpiece being a *Cenacolo* of matchless beauty. Our Saviour is standing in awful beauty and solemnity, and is about to administer the sacramental wafer, which He raises in one hand, while the other rests upon the beloved St. John, who bends beneath Him in ecstatic adoration; the other disciples lean breathlessly forward; in the foreground is the dark figure of Judas with his moneybag.

All around Valencia lies the Huerta, the most fertile district in Europe, and in the highest state of cultivation. Here lucerne is mown fifteen times in one year, and the rest of the crops are in proportion. Peas (January 20) were already in pod, and other vegetables in perfection. But the miasma from the stagnant waters — the whole course of the river being diverted for purposes of artificial irrigation—is unwholesome, and combined with the frequent sirocco, fresh from African deserts, renders the climate very depressing. We delighted to escape for one day by the railway to the more exhilarating air of Saguntum,—the old, well-known Roman name being that marked on our railway tickets, though the place is generally known in modern times as Murviedro.

is a wild and interesting place, a huge rock crowned with the remains of a Moorish castle, and clothed with prickly pear, and, on one of its sides, grand remains of a Roman theatre. While we were drawing, the simple, hospitable people crowded round us, full of eager questions as to England and other places of which they knew nothing, and peeled for us the delicious juicy cactus fruit. "Saguntum," they said, "was, next to Rome, the most important place in the world, and their Parróquia ranked only next to St. Peter's, on which account it had been decided that if the Holy Father should leave Rome, Saguntum was to be his residence. The Moors, who lived before the Romans, were the founders of Saguntum, and the ruined theatre was their Plaza de Toros."

We broke the long land journey to Alicante by sleeping at Jativa, which is just beyond the bounds of a lovely garden about ten miles' wide, which separates the Huerta from the stony deserts of inland Spain. Here the boughs of the orange-trees swept the carriage windows as we passed, and the vibrations of the train shook off showers of the over-ripe golden fruit. Groves of palms, often gathered around solitary, desolate *cartujas*, bent and rustled in the breeze. Jativa itself is full of fountains—a perfect city of clear rushing waters—and its bright little Alameda is fragrant with fruit and flowers. Behind the town, the mountain-side is full of hermitages and chapels, built amid groves of old carouba-trees and thickets of prickly pear. Altogether, it is a place one would like to linger in; but the extreme wretchedness of the inn drove us across the dismal plains, seven hours, to Alicante, where there is an excellent hotel (Bossio), one of the best in Spain.

This is, however, the best thing about the place—this and the climate—for Alicante is one of the driest places in the world. Not a particle of vegetation is to be seen, except the palm-trees on its Alameda. Everything has an Eastern look. The flat-roofed houses, the roads, the tawny, desolate plains which stretch around for miles and miles, are alike dust-coloured. The huge castle-crowned mass which overhangs the town and port is scarcely a rock, it is rather an immense dust-heap. Yet, even here, sunshine and shadow can work their ever-changing miracles, and can send great purple shadows across the mountains, which change their drab steeps, as by an enchanter's wand, and clothe them with colours of sapphire and amethyst. A small English colony exists at

CASTLE OF ALICANTE.

Alicante, with a consul, a chaplain, and a pleasant, hospitable little society. They told us that if we stayed long, we should learn to delight in the place, and even to think it beautiful; but to us it appeared so miserably abject and squalid, we could not believe it possible.

The drive from Alicante to Elche was our first experience of a Spanish diligence. We thought its discomforts greatly exaggerated, as the speed is far greater in proportion than that of the railway, without the trial to one's patience of perpetual unnecessary pottering at the small stations, which occur every five minutes. On the outside, the fresh air blowing over the vast plains was delightful, and the old Arragonese coachman in his quaintly decorated velveteen suit, with a large sombrero, vied in civilities with the Valencian *mayoral*. "To the right; to the left; go on, you creatures; Ave Maria Purisima, more to the left, you first one; go along with God, you outsider;" thus they talk to their horses, in a loud, stormy voice. There is very little guidance used, literally no driving at all; the horses hear and obey, or if the leader takes advantage of his distance, far beyond the reach of whip, to become wilful, stones are thrown at his tail, from a little hillock prepared all ready on the coach-box,—the object of which, on setting out, had greatly puzzled us.

After two hours' drive, a serrated line of palms rose upon the horizon, and soon we entered their forests. Far in the air, sometimes sixty feet high, rose the beautiful fans, with their enormous pendent bunches of dates, the golden fruit hanging from stems of so gorgeous an orange, that no mere description of colour can give the faintest idea of their effect when they are lighted up by the sun, and backed by a deep blue sky, as we first saw them. Their variety also is most beautiful: some of the older trees growing perfectly straight, others bending in the most picturesque attitudes, some buttressed up with little stone walls, and beside them younger palms rising in full youthful vigour, tens upon tens of thousands, for miles around.

Only the female trees bear fruit, and this only when they are impregnated with dust from the males, which is consequently done artificially. The male palms are often tied up and blanched to be cut for the Palm-Sunday festivals, and they are also sold to be stuck up in balconies as a protection against lightning, being considered quite as efficacious, and being certainly much cheaper, than an iron conductor. £2,000 worth are sold annually in Elche for this purpose, and £14,000 worth of dates. The latter were being gathered during our visit (January) by the clever little *hortelanos* who climb the branchless trunk like cats, a rope being passed round it and their waists, upon which they rest their whole weight in a horizontal position, lowering their baskets when filled, and raising them again by a pulley. The defective palm-leaves are sent to the manufactories and used as cigarettes. By the road-side, before every cottage-door, are quantities of dates in baskets, no one watching them; any passer-by can eat as many as he likes, fill his pockets, and leave his halfpenny in payment. It is generally left, for where Spaniards are trusted they scarcely ever abuse a trust. When we walked in the groves the hospitable peasants were only too anxious to load us with branches of the best fruit, and would accept no payment at all.

We spent three days in Elche, which, though the Roman Illica, is completely Moorish in character. There is a humble but decent posada. Ever-increasing was our delight in the enchanting walks; sometimes through the thick groves of magnificent date-palms, where all is richness and splendour of colour; sometimes in the deep brown ravine of the dried-up Vinalapo, which reminded us of the Valley of Jehoshaphat,—Elche, entirely Moorish, rising above like Jerusalem, with its flat-roofed houses, old walls, and crowning mosque; sometimes by the banks of little streams bordered with prickly pear and pomegranates; and sometimes out upon the desolate gravelly plain beyond all these, which assumes a wonderful colour towards sunset, and where the extreme clearness of the air makes the most distant objects, even to the violet mountains on the horizon, appear supernaturally distinct.

It is across a mere track in this plain that you set forth in the Murcia diligence, a track so ill-defined, so broken by large stones and even rocks, that an overturn seems inevitable every minute. Sometimes you reach the brink of an abandoned stone-quarry; further progress seems impossible, but the mayoral shouts and cracks his whip, down go the leaders by the merest semblance of a road, the lumbering diligence tumbles after, and at the bottom the horses just shake themselves and scramble on again not a bit the worse. But the road improves as it reaches Orihuela, an old cathedral city, where all the handsome girls were

AT ELCHE

walking about with fresh roses stuck jauntily behind their ears, and where the country is so excessively fertile that an old proverb says, whether it rains or not, corn will grow in Orihuela— "Llueva or no llueva, trigo in Orihuela." Merrily, with jangling bells, we drove on through the starlight to Murcia (Hotel Peregrino), a pleasant place with an interesting Gothic cathedral, and one of the most especially Moorish places in Spain, said, from the stagnation of its long existence, to be the only place Adam would recognise if he returned to earth.

Here we have heard the bell ringing through the streets and the people joining in singing the Rosario de la Aurora, so called because it is sung at dawn for the benefit of the souls in purgatory. This is a verse of it:—

> "En el Cielo se reza un Rosario
> Todas las mañanas al amanecer,
> Santiago lleva el estandarte,
> San Pedro la luz, la cruz San Miguel.
> Pues vamos allá,
> Que no hay cosa mas santa y mas dulce
> Que el Santo Rosario que se vá á rezar."

In Murcia we take leave of the eastern coast (for Cartagena is not worth visiting), with much gratitude for the enjoyment it has afforded us. No one who has not seen it can imagine the changes of scene it offers, the pictures it enables one to store up in one's mental gallery. The climate is delicious, not the burning sun by day with the cold frosty nights of a Roman winter, which send you to shiver in the evenings over a hopeless wood fire, but the clear equable bracing warmth of a fine early English September. Since the New Year to the present date (Feb. 2), we have had no rain. But what has most surprised us has been the exceeding facility of travelling and the charm of the treatment we have met with. We have quite laid aside now all thought of the mistrust which is a necessary habit in Italy. The fixed prices of the different hotels, which include board as well as lodging, prevent all trouble and preclude all notion of bargaining; and, whether in a first-rate fonda or a humble posada, you are received and treated, not as mere customers, but like honoured and welcome guests at a country house; and, being so treated, you learn to behave as such. The master of the house is your friend, who considers himself as your equal, and invariably expects to be shaken hands with on taking leave; the waiters and chamber-men (there are scarcely ever any female servants in Spanish hotels) are also your friends, but at a more respectful distance. Cheating and extortion seem incompatible with the Spanish character. Even the poorest peasant who has shown us our way, and who has walked a considerable distance to do so, has invariably refused to receive anything for his services; yet all are most willing and anxious to help strangers. The same liberal spirit seems to breathe through everything, and was equally shown at our little posada at Elche—equivalent to a small English public-house—where a number of maimed, blind, and halt collected daily to receive the broken viands from the table-d'hôte, which the mistress distributed to them, and in the delicate blacksmith's wife opposite, who keeps two lamps burning nightly at her own expense, before the little shrine of "Our Lady of the Unprotected" in her balcony. The temporal works of mercy—to give bread to the hungry, and drink to the thirsty, to take care of the sick, to visit the captives, and to bury the dead, these are the common duties which none shrink from.

As I write, a handsome dark-eyed brown boy in rags, who looks as if he had stepped out of one of Murillo's pictures, is leaning against the opposite wall in the moonlight, watching a shrine of the Virgin. It is a picture typical of Spain, ruined and superstitious, but still most beautiful—and so is the cry of the watchman which is ringing through the silent air, "Ave Maria Santisima, it is a quarter to twelve o'clock."

VI.

CORDOVA.

Fonda Rizzi, Cordova, *February* 8, 1872.

IT is a tremendous railway journey of twenty-two hours from Murcia to Cordova, with many disagreeable changes at miserably ordered stations, and no decent stopping place on the way. At Albacete, picturesquely-dressed men step into the carriage out of the midnight darkness, hung all round with knives with inlaid handles, and the daggers which are so indispensable to the costume of the *majo* or peasant dandy, and which are generally worn sticking out of the breeches-pocket. They are frequently adorned with mottoes, generally indicative of the savage service for which they are intended—the object of a Spanish knife being "to chip bread and kill a man." An immense number of people are employed in their manufacture at Albacete, which is bombastically called the Sheffield of Spain, and they are always sold at the station.

In the morning the train plodded—for a Spanish train never hurries—through La Mancha, the Don Quixote country, still almost as wild and uncultivated as in the days when the famous knight rode over its dull and desolate plains. Towards midday these were exchanged for green fields, and low hills clothed with cork trees, till at length the welcome towers of Cordova appeared, and an omnibus conveyed us along a bright Alameda garden, and then through the narrow streets, in which it often touches the houses on either side, till it could proceed no further, and disgorged its contents at the mouth of a street too narrow for any but foot passengers, leading to the Hôtel Rizzi.

The narrow streets, or rather alleys, so well adapted to give a shade in summer, when the heat here is almost insupportable, are an unaltered relic of the Moorish dominion, under which Cordova was the successful rival of Bagdad and Damascus. Utterly devoid of picturesqueness, they have a more thoroughly African appearance than those of any other town in Spain. One threads one's way between interminable whitewashed walls, their scanty windows guarded by heavy iron bars,

CORDOVA.

over a pebbly pavement so rough that it is like the bed of a torrent, littered with straw from the burdens of innumerable donkeys. There are no shops apparent, no animation whatever, nor any sign of life in the houses, and the few silent figures you pass are only miserable beggars wrapped in their mantas, generally lying on steps in the sun, almost too inert to extend their hands for charity, an occasional veiled lady gliding by to mass, or a majo, who goes swiftly along, erect upon his tall mule. Cordova is like a city of the dead; yet it looks modern and fresh, for every mark of antiquity is effaced by the coating of whitewash which clothes everything, and which makes the building of a thousand years ago undistinguishable from that of yesterday.

The little life which remains all seems to converge to the mosque, the one centre of interest in the town, the magnet which still attracts travellers to this whited sepulchre from all parts of the world. Here, in the magnificent court of oranges, troops of children play, a spectacle for a perfect regiment of beggars, who sun themselves all day long on the low stone seats around its walls, while crowds of strong able-bodied men stand here for hours gossiping and playing at cards—for at Cordova Spanish idleness reaches its climax. If a man wants a few pesetas he earns them; but when he has earned them he does not work again till they are spent, and as a Cordovan can live luxuriously on an orange, a piece of dried fish, and an air on the guitar, plenty of time is left to *flancur* and amuse themselves. And for this what spot can be more delightful than the grand old court, surrounded by flame-shaped battlements, entered by rich Moorish gateways, and where the fountain erected by Abdur-r-rahman in 945 still sends forth its volume of crystal waters beneath huge orange-trees planted some three hundred years ago, and above which feathery palms and tall cypresses shoot up into the clear air?

Oftentimes a group of the loiterers forms round one who is singing in a loud shrill voice, not very suitable for the consecrated precincts of a cathedral, some such snatches as this:—

"Los calzones del padre
De Catalina
Tienen cincuenta varas
Sin la pretina;"

or,—

"Mi marido se murió
Dios en el cielo le tenga;
Y le tenga tan tenido
Que nunca por acá vuelva;"

or, with a quaint look towards the stranger,—

> "Los enemigos del alma
> Todos dicen que son tres.
> Y yo digo que son cuatro
> Desde que conozco á usted."

From the court you step with bewilderment into a roofed-in forest of pillars, where you may truly lose your way amid the thousand still remaining columns (there were twelve hundred once) of varied colour, thickness, and material, which divide the building into twenty-nine naves one way and nineteen the other. Into the midst of all a cathedral was engrafted in 1547, for which many of the columns were destroyed, permission having been extorted by the canons from Charles V., who was unaware of the mischief they were doing, but who bitterly reproved them when he visited their work for having thus injured what was unique in the world. A tiny chapel, with a roof like a shell, formed from a single block of marble, is ornamented outside with mosaics sent from Constantinople by the Emperor Romanus II., the finest in the world. This is the Ceca, where the Alcoran was kept, as in a Holy of Holies; and at the opposite chapel of the Maksurah, also a beautiful remnant of Moorish times, though its pavement of pure silver has disappeared, the kalif performed his *chotba* or public prayer, at the Mihrab, a window looking towards the shrine. Just outside their sacred Ceca now stands, as if in mockery, the tomb of the Conde de Oropesa, who defended Cordova against the Moors in 1368. The only other especial object of interest shown is a scratch of the Crucifixion on a wall, attributed to the nails of a Christian captive; but the mosque may be visited in all hours and all lights with increasing wonder and delight.

Close below the mosque flows the broad Guadalquiver, here crossed by a fine old bridge, at the entrance of which is one of the]most beautiful artistic compositions in Cordova, where a huge brown gateway forms the background for the gaudy groups of country people, who wait with their mules, while their burdens are being examined at the barrier. It is a most animated scene, the mules kicking, struggling, and crowding on one another, the drivers gesticulating, shouting, and singing. Close by, the picturesque ruins of some Moorish mills, with open horse-shoe arches, stride out into the water. Behind, on a tall pillar, stands the statue of St. Raphael, the archangel, the protector of Cordova, an office which he swore to undertake, when he appeared to the Cordovan priest Andrès Roëlas, on the 7th of May, 1578, in the words which we may still read beneath his column.

> " Yo te juro por Jesu Cristo cruzificado
> Que soy Rafaël angel, á quien Dios tiene puesto
> Por guarda de esta ciudad."

An excursion should be made from Cordova to the picturesquely situated hermitages of the Sierra-Morena, a small Thebaid, about four miles distant, which may be accomplished on mules. There, or near where the hermitages now stand, was once situated the most magnificent of the Moorish buildings of Cordova, the city-like palace of Azzahra, built by the Khalif Annasir in honour of his wife, who begged that he would build a city for her which should be called by her name. It was begun A.D. 936, and was constructed by architects from Bagdad and Constantinople, 10,000 men, 2,400 mules, and 100 camels, being employed in the work. The palace contained 4,312 pillars of different kinds of precious marble; its hall called the Khalafat, had eight doors overlaid with gold and encrusted with precious stones, hung in arches of ebony and ivory; in the hall called Almunis was a great fountain brought from Constantinople, decorated with many figures of animals made of pure gold adorned with precious stones, with the water streaming from their mouths. When the palace was completed it was universally allowed that the whole land of Islam contained nothing to compare to it, that it passed the powers of language to describe. During the twenty-five years in which Annasir inhabited it, the annual expense was 300,000 dinars, and the number of its servants was 13,750 males, and 6,314 females, besides 3,750 Schlavonians. The miracles of art at Azzahra were totally destroyed in 1009; even the exact site of the palace is unknown, but the surrounding country still retains traces of the beautiful gardens of fruit trees by which it was surrounded by its founder. The ride to the hermitages is a lonely one, brigands are not absolutely unknown, and some little dread may be experienced at the sight of armed figures approaching down the narrow wooded paths. Generally, however, you are passed with the friendly Spanish salutation: "Dios guarde à usted!" "Va usted con Dios, caballero!" "God guard you, God be with you, sir."

VII.

SEVILLE.

Fonda Europa, Seville, *February* 21, 1872.

A PLEASANT railway journey of four hours brought us from Cordova to Seville. Long before reaching it, the famous Giralda tower appeared above the green corn plains, divided by hedges of aloes, and as the railway runs close under the town, between it and the Guadalquiver, all the principal buildings are seen before you arrive at the station. The tiresome and useless delay of the local custom-house, which worries travellers at the entrance of almost all the large Spanish towns, made it nearly dark when we reached the Fonda Europa, a thoroughly national hotel, with a court of oranges and a fountain, but exceedingly gloomy. Here, as elsewhere, we have often amused ourselves by thinking what a false idea people must entertain of places who only read of them in books. It is so easy to give a glowing picture of that which is dismal enough in reality, and from those who see the original the impression of the picture vanishes for ever. Thus O'Shea's really excellent guide-book, quite the best, we think, practically, though Ford—the original, unadulterated Ford—should on no account be left behind, writes of Valencia :—" The sultana of the Mediterranean cities, robed in the loose and sparkling white of her straggling houses, lies softly embosomed amid high palms and deep-green oranges, with her feet lazily bathing in the blue waves of the sea. The magic Huerta which surrounds her is but a large orchard," &c. How delightful an impression of dust-laden, wind-stricken dead-alive Valencia, three miles from the sea, with its three or four unhealthy palms, and its surrounding marshes and nursery gardens, which Murray further glorifies by describing their mud huts (*quintas*) as " pearls set in emeralds!" Even the truest picture is often misleading; for in writing from Seville I might say with perfect truth that I look down from my window through marble colonnades, bathed and glittering in the bright moonlight, perfumed with the scent of ancient orange and citron trees, which bend, fruit-laden, over a richly-sculptured fountain, while many birds of strange plumage flit amid their boughs, and golden fish float beneath the waters. Yet I should only be describing an ordinary Sevillian house, in which the bird-fancying landlord has clipped the wings of a number of hawks and owls, who live amid his orange-trees, and frighten his inmates by unexpectedly hopping in through their bedroom windows.

From the deathlike stillness of Cordova it is a strange transition to the animation and bustle of the central part of Seville, with its brilliant shops and crowded streets, in which you would think that the whole population amused themselves all day long. Of all the inhabitants of Spain, the Sevillians have the greatest reputation for liveliness of character and enjoyment of all the pleasures which the world can afford them. The past and the future seem to have no part in their existence; the present is everything. The churches here are deserted by comparison with those of other towns; the theatres and promenades are crowded. When we arrived the whole population was throwing itself rapturously into the delights of the carnival. The streets were filled every evening with masquers in every description of ridiculous dress, from Chinese mandarins and Indians in feathers to old English ladies with poke bonnets, reticule, and spectacles, and old English gentlemen with high collars, tail coats, and umbrellas, very admirably imitated. Reverence to the Church also was little evinced in the number of would-be nuns, mumbling over their breviaries, while their eyes, sparkling through their masques, sought a new object for a joke; and even the Pope himself had his representative, dragged woefully along by a horrible green devil with a long tail, which he lashed in glee over each contortion of the wretched potentate. In the carriages were many lovely little children of the nobles, beautifully dressed in blue, green, and yellow satin, à la Louis XIV., with their hair powdered, the little boys of three and four years old having silk stockings and buckles in their shoes. "Me conoces" resounded on all sides in the shrill voice of disguise which is universally adopted. All classes mingled together, and amused one another; yet at such times the high breeding and courtesy of every rank of Spaniard never deserts them, and no coarseness or breach of decorum can be discovered. At the same time, the unusual collision into which all persons are thrown is often produc-

SEVILLE

tive of bloodshed, and the utter *insouciance* about life which prevails in Spain was evidenced by the fact, that six persons were killed and eight wounded during the course of the first masqued ball, the long Albacete knives being used, and the murderers easily escaping in their masquerade dress, without its producing any effect upon the gaiety of the rest of the revellers.

With more than slightly sarcastic reference to the Italian king, who is much disliked here, the whole people of Seville, with banners flying, bands of music, and mounted troops of imaginary cavalry, went out to the gates at the beginning of carnival to meet the King of Nonsense, and solemnly escort him into the city, which he, a puppet, entered in a coach-and-four, bowing and nodding on either side from the windows, as real kings do. On the last day this figure was public deposed and executed— strangled as criminals are, on a scaffold in the great square, amid universal acclamations; and on the first Sunday in Lent (for the Sevillians, if robbed of some of their fun by the wet weather, use the Sundays in Lent for more carnival) tens of thousands of country people came into the town to see him lie in state, and attend his funeral with a procession of mock penitents, torches, and chanting. On other days of carnival *los gigantes*—huge figures of the Moorish sovereigns—were paraded round the town.

The people of Seville all seem proud now of its Moorish history, and aware of the advantages which that period has bequeathed to them. All the best Moorish houses are preserved, and the hot season of "the oven of Spain" is rendered endurable by the forethought which made the streets so narrow that it is generally impossible for two carriages to pass one another, while the houses which line them have large gardens, or are built round open courts, which, in summer, are covered with an awning or *velo*; while the windows are defended by the thick matted blinds called *esteras*. The names which are written up at the entrance of the streets in Seville are in themselves always picturesque and interesting, and have reference to events which occurred in them, or persons who have lived there. The word "calle," or street, is always omitted. The name stands alone—"Murillo," "Juan de Mena," "Abades," "Dados," &c. All are whitewashed, as at Cordova, and the clear shadows of the passers-by fall blue upon the dazzling walls. In the streets where most business is carried on, barriers are placed at each end of the

SEVILLE.

broad flagged pavement to prevent a carriage from attempting to enter, so that only mules and donkeys jostle the foot-passengers with their heavy burdens. Here the chief shops have no doors or windows, but are open porticos, supported on pillars, like oriental bazaars. Conspicuous among these are the shops of the gaily-coloured Mantas, generally kept by solemn-looking old Moors, who insist upon their customers being seated, and regale them with dates and sweetmeats, while they exhibit their wares; and those of the common earthenware, with their picturesque forms and bright green and red enamel. In the engravers' windows strangers will notice that some of the visiting-cards are black, with the name in white—these are the cards of the doctors, and, rather ominously, signify their calling.

If, in the evening, leaving the busier streets, filled far into the night with a moving crowd, amid which water-carriers are constantly circulating, with their shrill cry of "Agua, agua!" you turn into the quieter lanes flanked by private houses, you may generally see, not one, but many scenes, which look as if they were taken out of the play of *Romeo and Juliet*, of young men wrapped in their cloaks, clinging to the iron bars of one of the lower windows, making love, with the ripple of the fountain in the neighbouring patio as an accompaniment; only, at Seville, there is nothing surreptitious in this; it is the approved fashion of love-making, admitted by parents and guardians, and to neglect it on the part of the innamorato, would be to forfeit his lady's good graces. Fatal frays frequently occur in the streets, in consequence of the lover arriving and finding his place occupied by another. Often the love-making is no whispered confidence, but a serenade on the guitar. The verses sung are seldom original, and have a savour of Moorish times and imagery. Here are some of them:—

> "Tus colchones son jazmines
> Y tus sábanas mosquetas,
> Azucenas tu almohada,
> Y tú, rosa que te acuestas."

> "Los cipreses de tu casa
> Están vestidos de luto,
> Y es porque no tienen flores
> Que ofrecerte por tributo."

> "El naranjo de tu patio
> Cuando te acercas á él,
> Se desprende de sus flores
> Y te las echa á los piés."

> "Son tus labios dos cortinas
> De color de carmesí,
> Y entre cortina y cortina
> Estoy esperando el sí."

Looking into the patios of Sevillian houses is like looking into the private life of their inhabitants, for the adornment of each may be considered to reflect the taste of its owner; in one brilliant flowers, in another a marble fountain, or a beautiful statue, or drooping bananas, or tall palms, or cypresses clipped into strange forms of temples and pagodas. Here the *tertulias* are given, the pleasant, unformal receptions which are the only kind of evening parties in common use in Spain. When properly presented at any Spanish house, its master says to you on taking leave, after your first visit, "Henceforth this house is yours," and from that time you may come and go unrestrained, and feel sure that you are always welcome, though you are offered no refreshment, or only a cup of chocolate, which it is not usual to accept, and though the master of the house himself is seldom at home, being at some other tertulia. In the course of the evening, one of the gentlemen present often takes a guitar, then the younger guests dance, while their elders play at cards or gossip round the fountain. If a sudden silence falls upon the company it is attributed to the passing of an angel, who imposes upon the air, which is wafted by his wings, the respect of silence, without any definite cause or comprehension. With Spaniards dinner-parties are almost unknown; though invitations are sometimes given, it is a mere matter of form, which all well-bred persons are expected to refuse, unless pressed repeatedly. Great stress is laid upon all the formalities of Spanish courtesy, and a stranger is measured by his observation of them. It is absolutely necessary that a first visit at a Spanish house should be paid in complete black, though morning dress may be worn. The visitor's hat is then seized, the utmost consideration is paid to it, and it is solemnly placed on a cushioned chair by itself, and this attention must be carefully observed when the visit is returned. No attempt must be made to shut the doors, for to be alone with a lady with closed doors would be considered indecorous, and it must be remembered that Spanish ladies never either shake hands or take a gentleman's arm; but when the visitor rises, he must say, "Beso los pies de usted, señora"— ("Lady, I kiss your feet;") to which the lady responds, "Beso á usted la mano, caballero"—" Sir, I kiss your hand.") Religious topics can seldom be touched upon with impunity, for the mass of Spaniards consider Protestants little better than heathen, a belief which is very naturally fostered by the extremely irreverent behaviour of our countrymen in Roman Catholic churches, and by their habit of walking about looking at the pictures and statues, and talking aloud, even at the most solemn moments of the services. Here, though the spirit may be overlocked, scrupulous attention is paid to the letter of the national religion, which is nowhere more perceptible than in the universal impulse with which all classes alike fall at once on their knees when the tinkling of a little bell announces that the Sacrament is being carried past. An old proverb says, with regard to genuflecture—"Al Rey, en viendole; á Dios en oyendole." Even at a theatre, in the midst of a performance, if this bell is heard, actors and audience alike fall upon their knees till it ceases. The Sacrament, like the king, is spoken of as "Su Majestad." Thus when, after prayer, the consecrated wafer is placed in the mouth of a dying person, a priest, after a few minutes, approaches with a napkin, and asks, "Ha pasado su Majestad?" ("Has his Majesty gone down?")

"Quien no ha visto Sevilla,
No ha visto maravilla,"

is a proverb which its inhabitants delight in, but which may equally be applied to many of the other towns of Spain. To the seeker after the picturesque, Seville must unavoidably be a disappointment. The first view even of the famous cathedral is a shock. It has no external beauty, and cannot compare with any of the great French cathedrals, or even with many of the English ones. It stands on a high platform, girdled with pillars, partly brought from Italica, and partly relics of the mosques, of which two existed on this site. The last, built by the Emir Yusuf in 1184, was pulled down 1401, when the cathedral was begun, only the Giralda, the Court of Oranges, and some of the outer walls being preserved. The Chapter, when convened for the building of the cathedral, determined, like religious Titans, to build one "of such size and beauty that coming ages should proclaim them mad for having undertaken it." To their efforts the main portion of the edifice is due, paid for chiefly out of their own incomes, but so many chapels and dependent offices have been added, that even on the exterior every phase of architecture is represented — Gothic, Moorish, Græco-Roman, Revival, and Plateresque; while in the interior every century has erected a chapel or retablo in its own peculiar style.

Far above houses and palaces, far above the

huge cathedral itself, soars the beautiful Giralda, its colour a pale pink, encrusted all over with delicate Moorish ornament; so high that its detail is quite lost as you gaze upward; so large that you may easily ride on horseback to the summit, up the broad roadway in the interior. The lower part of the tower alone is really Moorish; the upper tier, with the bells and the surmounting cupolas, was added by Francesco Ruiz in 1568, who inscribed his work with the large letters, "Turris fortissima nomen Dei." At the summit is a figure of Faith, inappropriately chosen to turn with every wind of heaven, executed by Bartolomé Morel. Nothing can be more enchanting than to spend a morning at the top of this tower, where from the broad embrasures, you overlook the whole city, the soft bends of the Guadalquiver, and the sunny green plains melting into an amethystine distance. Subdued by the height, the hum of the great city scarcely reaches you; but the chime of many bells ascends into the clear air, and mingles with the song of the birds, which are ever circling round the tower in the aërial space, and perching on the great lilies which adorn it. Just below are children, always playing in the Court of Oranges, where the old fountain, used in the Moorish ablutions, still sparkles in the sunshine.

It is perhaps best to enter the mighty cathedral from this courtyard, where you find the Puerta del Lagarto, so called from the crocodile which hangs above it, which was sent by the Sultan as a present when he asked for the daughter of Alonzo el Sabio as his wife. The king kept the gift, but declined the young lady, who thought that her lover's first present was scarcely indicative of the tender regard she expected.

The effect of the interior of the cathedral is terribly marred by the huge mass of the choir and the retablo of the high altar, which block up the view in every direction. In the former is an inscription, saying that "Nufro Sanchez, a sculptor, whom God held in his keeping, made this choir in 1475." Everything is vast, down to the paschal-candle, placed in a candlestick twenty-five feet high, and weighing 2,500 lbs. of wax, while the expenditure of the chapter may be estimated by the fact that 18,750 litres of wine are consumed annually in the sacrament. Of the ninety-three stained windows, many are old and splendid. Their light is undimmed by curtains, for there is an Andalusian proverb that the ray of the sun has no power to injure within the bounds in which the voice of prayer can be heard. In the centre of the nave, near the west door, surrounded by sculptured caravelas, the primitive ships by which the New World was discovered, is the tomb of Ferdinand Columbus, son of the great navigator (who himself rests in Havannah), inscribed—

> "A Castilla y á Leon
> Mundo nuevo dio Colon."

At the opposite end of the church is the royal chapel, where St. Ferdinand, who was canonised in 1627, "because he carried faggots with his own hands for the burning of heretics," rests beneath the altar in a silver sarcophagus. Here also are his Queen Beatrix, his son Alonzo el Sabio, father of our Queen Eleanor, and Maria de Padilla, the beautiful morganatic wife of Pedro the Cruel.

Every chapel is a museum of painting and sculpture; but amid such a maze of beauty three pictures stand forth beyond all others. The first is the "Angel de la Guarda" of Murillo, in which a glorious seraph with spreading wings leads a little trustful child by the hand, and directs him to look beyond earth into the heavenly light.

The second is the S. Antonio of Murillo, in the baptistery. The saint is represented kneeling in a cell, of which all the poor details are faithfully given, while the long arcade of a cloister can be seen through the half-open door. Above, in a transparent light, which flows from himself, the child Jesus appears, and descends, floating through wreaths of angels, drawn down by the power of prayer. The third is in the great sacristy; it is the solemn, awful "Deposition from the Cross," by Pedro de Campana, before which, by his own desire, Murillo was buried. In his lifetime he would remain for hours before this picture. The sacristan once asked him why he thus stood gazing there. "I am waiting, he said, "till those holy men have finished their work."

Many of the services in this church reach a degree of splendour which is only equalled by those of St. Peter's; and the two organs, whose gigantic pipes have been compared to the columns of Fingal's cave, peal forth magnificently. But one ceremony, at least, is far more fantastic than anything at Rome, when at Corpus Christi and the octave of the Immaculate Conception, the choristers *dance* before the altar with castanets, wearing plumed hats and a dress of the time of

Philip III., red and white for Corpus Christi, and blue and white for the Virgin.

Sermons are still occasionally preached in the open cloister, from the stone pulpit, whence S. Vicente Ferrer declaimed the horrors of the Inquisition, and most picturesque is the scene, of the vast congregation seated round the fountain, and under the shade of the old orange-trees. The gift of preaching has by no means perished out of Spain, and is still well represented in Seville. Perhaps the most celebrated preacher of late years in the Peninsula has been Don Cayetano Fernandez, a monk of the Oratory here, some of whose teachings have been published under the title of "Fabulas Asceticas." Their pictorial eloquence and imagery is well suited to the Spanish mind: see this fragment:—

"'O suffering! O cruelty!' thus cried an olive-tree, which an active hand was despoiling of its branches.

"'Why, by the edge of your bill-hook, do you thus cause my ruin? Is this your love for me, O gardener?

"'Already my shorn and injured head has ceased to offer either shade or beauty, in the midst of the pain which overwhelms me.'

"'Be silent! cease your importunate lamentations,' answered the man. 'That which is required of you is not beauty, or shade, it is olives.

"'You will see, in April, with how many flowers your poverty will be clothed, and the abundant harvest which you will give in October.

"'Until that time, O olive, have patience.'

"Do you also, O Christian, adore the chastisement of a severe and inflexible Providence; it does but prepare through suffering the fruits of autumn."

Or this :—

"'Penelope, many persons call me a Penelope; it enrages me to hear it. Why do they treat me so ill?'—'Because your life is spent in *spinning* and *unspinning*.'

"Do you not know that the Lady Penelope passed her days in spinning her web, and that, in the night, she unravelled it? This is why the name is given to all women who imitate her—who *spin* and *unspin*.

"The young girl who thinks herself religious, who goes to mass and sermon, and who at night, at parties, dances the fango and gavotta, is occupied, in my opinion, in *spinning* and *unspinning*.

"If she reads A Kempis and the Christian Year, and then has Dumas and Victor Hugo in her hands, it is (who cannot see it?) to *spin* and *unspin*.

"And if, a model daughter, she is like a slave in her obedience, yet gives *rendezvous* at the grille of her window and the crevice of her door, it is but the old story of *spinning* and *unspinning*.

"She who humbly kisses the earth, and, at the least insult, rises to become a fury; she who throws herself upon her enemy and tears her hair, has made terrible progress in the art of *spinning* and *unspinning*.

"She who rises early to go to confession, as I see more than one of you do, and who, in the evening, thinks of nothing but amusing herself at the theatre; what do you call that?—*spinning* and *unspinning*.

"And what when she welcomes the poor, because she loves to do good; if, at Tertulias, she backbites her neighbours, it is so much good lost. She has *spun* and *unspun*.

"And if, at a religious meeting, she recites the Short Litany and immediately goes to gallivant upon the Alameda at the expense of her modesty, she runs the risk of losing everything in *spinning* and *unspinning*.

"For to be an angel by day and a little devil by night, is to go with four horses to hell, is foolish and absurd, is to sow and not to reap, is . . . . . to *spin* and *unspin*."

The grass-grown squares to the north of the cathedral are surrounded by an interesting group of buildings of various dates. First comes the vast Lonja or Exchange, built 1582-98, enclosing a grand staircase of brown and red marble, and containing, on its upper floor, the precious correspondence of Columbus, Pizarro, and Fernando Cortes. Opposite this is the huge Archiepiscopal Palace of 1697.

Between these two buildings we approach the serrated walls of the famous Alcazar (Al Kasr—the house of Cæsar), which was begun in 1181, but in great part rebuilt by Pedro the Cruel (1353-64), and again altered by Charles V., who displayed here the same passion for building one palace inside another which has disfigured the Alhambra. Pedro, however, strictly imitated the Moorish sovereigns in his buildings, as he tried to resemble them by administering open-air justice in the Patio de las Banderas. The history of this strange monarch gives the Alcazar its chief interest. Hither he fled with his mother as a child from his father Alonzo XI. and his mistress, Leonora de Guzman. They were protected by the minister, Albuquerque, at whose house he met and loved Maria de Padilla, a Castillian beauty of noble birth, whom he secretly married. Albuquerque was furious, and aided by the queen-mother, forced him into a political marriage with the French princess, Blanche de Bourbon. He met her at Valladolid, but, three days after his nuptials, fled from the wife he disliked to the one he loved, who ever after held royal court at Seville, while Queen Blanche, a sort of Spanish Mary Stuart, after being cruelly persecuted and imprisoned for many years, was finally put to death at Medina-Sidonia. In this Alcazar also Pedro received the Red King of Granada, with a promise of safe conduct, and then murdered him for the sake of his jewels, one of which, a large ruby, which he gave to the Black Prince after Navarete, and which is "the fair ruby, great like a racket-ball," which Elizabeth showed to the ambassador of Mary of Scotland, now adorns the royal crown of England. Of his nocturnal adventures many strange stories are told. One is still quaintly commemorated in Seville. The king, cloaked and disguised, used to serenade his various loves, Seville-fashion, beneath their window-bars. One day, on arriving at a rendezvous, he found his place already occupied, and in a fit of jealousy he killed his rival. The only person who saw the deed was an old woman who was sitting up baking. In the murderer she recognised the king, but, fearing one whom all dreaded, she kept silence. The next day the news of the tragedy resounded through Seville. Pedro, imagining that no eye had seen the deed, sat upon his judgment-seat in the Banderas, sent for the alcalde of the town, and declared that his own head should answer for that of the murderer unless he produced him in three days. The terrified alcalde inquired of all people in the neighbourhood of the fatal spot, and at length found the old woman, who revealed the truth. But there was still the difficulty of accusing the awful king to his face. To meet it he made a puppet, which he painted and dressed exactly like the king, and when the three days expired he presented himself before Pedro, saying that he had found the murderer and captured him, and when Pedro declared his incredulity he produced the image. Then the king went through a mock form of trial, and condemned the image to death, and it was hung in chains at the entrance of the street ever since called Justicia, where the bust of Pedro may still be seen on the spot on which the murder was committed, as well as the Moorish house, unaltered, whence it was seen by the old woman. It was in the Alcazar also that Pedro murdered his illegitimate brother, the master of Santiago, who had caused him much trouble by a rebellion. Maria de Padilla knew his coming fate, but did not dare to tell him, though from the beautiful ajimez window over the gate, she watched for his arrival, and tried to warn him by her tears. Six years after, this murder was avenged by Henry of Trastamare, the brother of the slain, who stabbed Pedro to the heart; but Maria de Padilla was already dead, and buried with queens in the royal chapel, when Pedro publicly acknowledged her as his lawful wife, and the marriage received the sanction of the Spanish Church.

Over the door of the Alcazar is the device of El Nodo, in reference to the fidelity of Seville to Alonzo el Sabio. Within all is still fresh and brilliant with light and colour. It is like a scene from the Arabian Nights, or the wonderful creation of a kaleidoscope. The first court is called Las Donzellas, because there it is said that the Moorish sovereign used to choose his wives, fifty rich and fifty poor, all the young ladies of Seville passing in review for the purpose. The Hall of Ambassadors is perfectly glorious in its delicate lacelike ornaments and the rich colour of its exquisite azulejos. It has a "Naranja ceiling" like the inside of an orange. In one corner there are dark stains upon the floor. "Ah, blood!" said the old guide, "I know that word of English; it means sangre. All the English ladies who come here look for that stain, and then they say 'Blood!'" It is said to be that of the victim of Don Pedro, who called out, "Slay the master of Santiago!' from the upper gallery, beneath which his portrait and those of his two wives, opposite to one another, are let into the wall. Beyond this are shown the sleeping rooms of the Moorish king, where his four hundred wives and his three hundred children were accommodated—a number which seems less incredible when one learns that the present Emperor of Morocco has had eighty children born in one month!

On the upper floor is the bedchamber of Don Pedro, outside which still hang the skulls of some unjust judges which he caused to be placed there, that he might look upon them whenever he went in or out. Here also is a beautiful little chapel built by Isabella the Catholic, in which her grandson, Charles V., was married to Isabella of Portugal. The arms of the great Isabella are seen bound by a yoke to those of Ferdinand, whose jealousy added the motto, "Tanto monta," "One is as good as the other."

Behind the Alcazar, approached by a separate entrance, are its lovely gardens, laid out by Charles V., an absolute blaze of sunshine and beauty, where, between myrtle hedges and terraces lined with brilliant tulips and ranunculuses, fountains spring up on either side the path, and gradually rising higher and higher, unite, and dance together through the flowers. Beyond the more formal gardens are ancient orange-groves covered with fruit. The ground is littered with their golden balls. "There are so many," the gardener said, "it is not worth while to pick them up." We gathered as many as we liked, and felt that no one knew what an orange was who had not tasted the sunny fruit of Seville. One old tree is shown as having been planted by Don Pedro. It stands near the pleasant summer-house of Charles V., covered with purple azulejos. His bath is also shown beneath the orange bowers, and that of Maria de Padilla, an arched crypt, delightful in summer, with a hole through which Pedro could look down at her. In another part of the garden are twenty-nine hideous camels, pets of poor Queen Isabella, which the new government tried to sell, and, when they failed, sent here to do what work they could.

Just behind the Alcazar is the Plaza S. Tomas, where Figaro, "the Barber of Seville," had his shop. It is strange that no enterprising barber should set up a shop there now.

Facing the pretty Botanical Garden near this is an enormous and stately building, which we at first imagined to be a royal palace, but afterwards found to be the Government tobacco manufactory, where six thousand women are employed daily. As they are paid according to the amount of work they do, all is activity and diligence, and it is astonishing to see the deftness with which the cigars are rolled up. Here the best types of Andalusian beauty may be seen. One part of the building is entirely devoted to the Gipsies, who carry on their separate dialect and sing their own songs here among themselves. Morality is at a low ebb:—

> "El hombre è fuego, la muger estopa,
> Viene el diablo y sópla."

Infants produce small scandal in Seville; they may be only the result of having eaten of the lily, which is sacred to the Virgin!

On the other side of the same garden rises another palace, really inhabited by royalty. It is that of S. Elmo, originally founded as a naval school by the companions of Columbus, in gratitude for having been saved during a tempest by the mariners' saint. His statue stands above the handsome portal, but his reputation is at a low ebb now, even at Naples, for he is always said to appear after the storm is over! Queen Isabella gave the building to her sister, the Duchesse de Montpensier, and since the revolution of 1848 she and her husband have made it their principal residence. They are exceedingly popular at Seville, where they do a great deal of good by careful and discriminating charity, to which they give much personal attention, and in encouragement of art and skill of every description. S. Elmo is a charming ideal of a happy family home. Its beautiful marble courts and halls, where a fountain often plays in the centre of each chamber, and in which are no fire-places, present too cold an aspect for our northern notions of comfort in winter; but in summer they must be delightful; and the walls are completely covered with family relics and *souvenirs*, evidently greatly prized and cared for. These include portraits of Louis Philippe, Marie Amelie, and Madame Adelaide, frequently repeated, with those of all the brothers and sisters of the Duke; pictures also of various family events—the baptism and marriage of the Comte de Paris, Louis Philippe and his five sons on horseback, &c. Among a number of sketches, evidently framed rather for the sake of the artists than for any intrinsic value of their own, is one "par la Princesse Alexandrine Victoire, fille du Duc de Kent; en 1835," representing an angel of mercy visiting a starving family. In the Duchess's room are many portraits of her own family—her sister, Queen Isabella, represented over and over again, the first time as a baby of a few months old; her mother, and Don Francisco d'Assisi, the queen's husband. The first hall is surrounded by glass-cases filled with little memorials of family tours—pottery from Etruria, glass and lamps from the Catacombs, coins, medals, and dried plants. In one of the rooms are the Madonna della Faja of Murillo and Ary Scheffer's beautiful picture of "Monica and Augustine." In a patio are copies of the tombs of two infantas who have died. When the first child died, it was buried in the royal chapel of the cathedral, but when the second died, and the parents wished to lay it there also, it was not allowed: "They were no longer royal; the royal chapel was not for them." It was the greatest insult which the Revolution offered them.

In front of S. Elmo rises the Torre del Oro, a river bastion of the Alcazar, once united to it by walls which were destroyed to make way for the promenade called the Christina. It was used as a prison for the disgraced mistresses of Don Pedro. Its name is said to be derived from the gilt tiles which once roofed it. These have now been taken away, but are amply compensated for, as far as the name goes, by the bright yellow wash with which the walls are covered.

Hence, along the bank of the muddy Guadalquiver, extends the pleasant promenade of Las Delicias, crowded in the afternoon with Sevillian beauties. On the promenade ladies often wear low dresses and their hair dressed with flowers, while even at a large evening party high dress is the rule. Every possible form and size of fan is to be seen— often with a handle, and so large that it is used as a parasol. There are fans for every season and for every occasion. A friend of ours asked a Spanish lady how many she had. "Only thirty dozen," she said, and thought it very few. In church, where there are no chairs or seats of any kind, and where all the ladies sit picturesquely upon the floor, the flapping of fans in the hot weather is prodigious. Many writers have dilated upon the beautiful feet of the Spanish ladies, but their dresses are worn so very long, that it is difficult to imagine how this knowledge can have been arrived at. Nor is this hiding of feet merely the result of modern fashion; the feet of Spanish ladies have always been concealed. Mediæval artists were always forbidden to paint the feet of the Virgin, and to mention them was as sacrilegious, as it was disloyal to allude to the possibility of the queens of Spain having legs.

The Hospital of the Caridad was founded by Don Miguel de Mañana, or Tenorio, a Don Juan of the seventeenth century. His story relates that when he was coming out from a midnight orgy, he encountered a funeral procession, with mutes and torches, and inquiring whose it was, was told that it was that of Don Miguel de Mañana, and in the corpse they bore beheld with horror his own image. The bearers said that they were about to celebrate the funeral mass, and bade him accompany them, and join them in praying for the soul of Don Miguel. He did so, and the following morning was found senseless upon the floor of the church. From that time his career was changed, he sought only works of charity and mercy, and at his death endowed this hospital with ten thousand pounds a year, commanding that he should be buried at the church-door, so that all who passed by might trample on his grave, which by his own direction bears the epitaph, "Here lies the worst man in the world."

When we went to see the pictures we asked for the sacristan, and were told, "Here the sacristan is una Madre de Caridad." These sisters manage the whole, and take care of a hundred and forty old men in a well-organized hospital, the wards consisting of two long galleries, divided by pillars.

The small church contains a wonderful collection of pictures. The six Murillos include his two famous large representations of Moses striking the rock and the miracle of the loaves and fishes. The grand and affecting altar-piece of the Deposition is by Pedro Roldan, with a background painted by Valdes Leal. Near the door, by the same artist, is the too truthful picture of "Los Dos Cadaveres," before which Murillo used to hold his nose.

The picture-gallery in the Convento de la Merced is almost filled with the works of Murillo. Eight of his finest pictures were painted for the glorious retablo of the Capuchin convent, closed in 1835, and of these seven are now here. Perhaps the gem of the whole collection is the St. Thomas of Villanueva, Murillo's own favourite picture, which he called "Mi Cuadro." St. Thomas was the favourite preacher of Charles V., and was created Archbishop of Valencia, where he seemed to spend the whole of his revenues in charity, yet never contracted any debt; so that his people used to believe that angels must minister to his temporal wants. He is represented at his cathedral door, distributing alms, robed in black, with a white mitre. A poor cripple kneels at his feet, and other mendicants are grouped around. Near this, hangs the grand picture of the Vision of St. Francis of Assisi, to whom the Saviour visibly descends from the crucifix. St. Francis turns to receive his Lord with awe and love unspeakable, and, as he turns, the world, represented by a globe, rolls away from beneath his feet. "La Virgen de la Servilleta" is a lovely small picture, which derives its name from having been painted on a napkin. When Murillo was working at the convent, the cook entreated to have something as a memorial, and presented a napkin as the canvas, on which this brilliant, glowing Madonna was painted, with a Child which seems quite to bound forward out of the picture.

One other building in Seville deserves especial mention. It is the Casa de Pilatos, the palace of the Dukes of Medina Celi, built by a Marquis of Tarifa on his return from Palestine in 1520, in professed imitation of the house of Pilate at Jerusalem. To render this resemblance complete, nothing has been omitted, the Prætorium, the pillar of the scourging, the basin in which the hands were washed, the table where the thirty pieces of silver were counted, while at the top of the stairs the cock which crowed is seen, stuffed, in a niche, with entire disregard of the fact that this famous bird lived in the house, not of Pilate, but Caiaphas. But the real interest of the house is derived from its splendid azulejos, like those of the Alcazar, the gorgeous purple colour of its tiled staircase, and its little garden of enormous bananas.

One lovely evening we drove out to Italica, passing through the gipsy quarter of Triana, where Murillo studied his ragged boys, and where pots are still sold like those which Santa Rufina and Santa Justina were making on this spot, where they were stoned to death for refusing to bow down to the image of Venus. Murillo, when he painted his famous picture of the sainted tutelars, took as his models two peasant-girls of Triana.

Here is a church with the strange name of "Sant' O." Beyond Triana, a dreadfully bad road leads across the green corn-covered plain to the foot of a low line of hills, where are to be found the few vestiges which mark the site of the city where the emperors Trajan, Hadrian, and Theodosius, were born. Even the "ruins of the ruins" were destroyed by the earthquake of 1755. Enough of the amphitheatre alone remains to show the former importance of the place. When we saw it, the broad area was filled with water, in which the ruined seats were reflected as in a mirror. We sate to sketch the lovely effect as sunset bathed the whole with gold, and introduced the figure of the old guide, seated on a rocky fragment; "thus he would live on after he was dead," he said. His cottage clings to the ruins like a parasite, shaded by a huge fig-tree, and in all the rugged interstices around he has planted roses, mignonette, and coronella, so that it is a perfect bower of sweets. The only other inhabitants of Italica are vast bands of black pigs, which live in its vaulted passages.

On a neighbouring hillock is the fine old neglected convent of S. Isidoro, gutted by Soult. Its church contains a beautiful statue of the patron saint, by Montanes, and the tombs of Guzman el Bueno and his family. This Guzman received his surname from King Sancho el Bravo, after the defence of Tarifa against the Moors. He had entrusted his eldest son, of nine years old, to the care of the Infante Juan, who leagued with the Infidels, and who brought the child under the walls, threatening to kill him if the fortress was not surrendered. Guzman replied, "I prefer honour without a son, to a son with dishonour;" and the boy was killed. When, called by the cry of horror to the battlements, Guzman saw his child's dead body, he turned to its mother, saying calmly, "I feared that the infidel had taken the city." The daughter-in-law of Guzman, Doña Uriaca Osorio, who is also buried here, was burnt alive by Pedro the Cruel, for refusing to become his mistress. Her epitaph also records the fate of her faithful maid Leonora Davalos, who insisted upon dying with her beloved mistress. As we emerged from the dark convent courts we came upon one of those striking views so completely Spanish in character, and which derive all their charm from its climate. In the distance, against faint blue mountains, the cathedral and town rose through a violet mist, then came the rich green plains, intersected by long fiords of water; and on the rich dark Siena foreground, groups of gaily-dressed peasants, with their hundreds of pigs, stood out in the strongest relief of shadow against the brilliant sunset-colour. Fernando Cortes died hard by (December 9, 1597), at Castillejo de la Cuesta (now a country house of the Montpensiers), where Bernal Diaz says that he sought retirement for the purpose of making his will and preparing his soul for death; "and when he had settled his worldly affairs, our Lord Jesus Christ was pleased to take him from this troublesome world." He was first buried at S. Isidoro, but his remains were afterwards removed to Tezcuco, in New Spain.

Our last visit at Seville was to the site of the Quemadero, on the plain called Prado San Sebastian, outside the walls; where, and in the Plaza San Francisco, beneath the picturesque old Casa del Ayuntamiento, the *autos da fé* took place. The bricks of the long-used scaffold, where so many suffered, can only just be seen peeping through the grass beneath which time has so long been burying them. But here, that which Bossuet describes as "the holy severity of the Church of Rome, which will not tolerate error," burnt 34,601 persons alive, and 18,043 persons in effigy, between 1481 and

1700, besides imprisoning and sending to the galleys many thousands of others. In all cases the property of the sufferers was confiscated and their families left destitute. It can scarcely be wondered at that Seville is now foremost among Spanish cities in her search after a reformed faith. Many Protestant schools are opened, in which about four hundred children are being educated; and though they are preached against in the cathedral, and denounced from the pulpit of St. Vincent Ferrer, their teachers are gladly welcomed and universally treated with respect by the people. The church of S. Basilio has been bought from the Roman Catholics, and services are performed and sermons preached there in Spanish. When the building was being repaired by its new possessors, its roof was found to be full of the bones of children. Even at the English services Spaniards of the lower classes often appear, and behave reverently.

VIII.

CADIZ AND GIBRALTAR.

KING'S ARMS HOTEL, GIBRALTAR, *March* 11.

ON February 22nd we left Seville for Cadiz. For more than an hour before reaching it, the town rises over the flats, but the railway has to make a long circuit, following all the windings of the bay. Here are productive saltpans, called by religious titles, such as "Il dulce nombre de Jesus," which seems profane; yet, as Ford observes, is perhaps not more so than the familiar use in Oxford of such names of colleges as Corpus, Jesus, Trinity, and Christ Church. The distant effect of the white town rising above the deep blue waters is most brilliant and dazzling, and within its narrow streets it is impossible to get away from the glare of the whitewash, of which every building receives a fresh coating annually. The high sea-wall is the only pleasant walk, with its little gardens full of bright scarlet geraniums and hedged with heliotrope and ixias. Here we may spend a hot afternoon very agreeably, and study Spanish life and manners, or listen to the numerous nursery maids who are singing to their children such verses as:—

> "A la nana le cantaba
> La Virgen á sus amores!
> Dulce hijo de mi vida,
> Perdona á los peccadores
>
> A la puerta del cielo
> Venden zapatos
> Para los angelitos
> Que estan descalzos.
>
> Todo lo chiquitito
> Me hace á mi gracia
> Hasta los pucheritos
> De media cuarta.
>
> El niño de Maria
> No tiene cuna,
> Su padre es carpintero
> Y le hará una.
>
> Niño chiquirrito
> De pecho y cuna
> Dónde estará tu madre
> Que no te arrulla."

In one of the convents of Cadiz is the picture of the marriage of St. Catherine, in painting which Murillo fell from his scaffold, and received the injuries of which he died. But there is literally nothing else to see in Cadiz, and as the land road, which we had intended taking, was rendered quite impracticable by the recent rains, we were glad to find a steamer leaving next morning for Algeciras, opposite Gibraltar.

It was a lovely day, and a calm sea, which was a great subject of rejoicing, for even as it was the rickety Spanish vessel rolled disagreeably. Owing to the miserable slowness of everything, we were eleven hours on board. There was little interest till we reached the yellow headland of Trafalgar. Then the rugged outlines of the African coast rose before us, and we entered the straits, between Tarifa sleeping amid its orange groves on the Spanish coast, and the fine African peak above Ceuta. Soon, on the left, the great rock of Gibraltar rose from the sea like an island, though not the most precipitous side, which turns inwards towards the Mediterranean. But it was already gun-fire, and too late to join another steamer and land at the town, so we waited for a shoal of small boats which put out from Algeciras, and surrounded our steamer to carry us on shore.

Here we found in the Fonda Inglesa (kept by an English landlady), one of the most primitive but charming little hotels we ever entered. The view from our rooms alone decided us to stay there some days. Hence, framed by the balcony, Gibraltar rose before us in all the glory of its rugged sharp-edged cliffs, grey in the morning, pink in the evening light, with the town at its foot, whence, at night, thousands of lights were reflected in the still water. In the foreground were groups of fishing-boats at anchor, and, here and there, a lateen sail flitted, like a white albatross, across the bay. On the little pier beneath us was endless life and movement, knots of fishermen, in their blue shirts and scarlet caps and sashes, mingling with solemn-looking Moors, in turbans, yellow slippers, and flowing burnouses, who were watching the arrival or embarkation of their wares; and an endless variety of travellers from all parts of Europe, waiting for different steamers, or come over to see the place. Here an invalid might stay, imbibing health from the fine air and sunshine, and never be weary of the ever-changing diorama. In every direction delightful walks wind along the cliffs through groves of aloes and prickly-pear, or descend into little sandy coves full of beautiful shells. Behind the town, a fine old aqueduct strides across the valley, and beyond it the wild

GIBRALTAR, FROM ALGECIRAS.

moors begin at once sweeping backwards to a rugged chain of mountains. Into the gorges of these mountains we rode one day, and most delightful they are, clothed in parts with magnificent old cork-trees, while in the depths of a ravine, overhung with oleander and rhododendron, is a beautiful waterfall.

It was with real regret that we left Algeciras and made the short voyage across the bay to Gibraltar, where we instantly found ourselves in a place as unlike Spain as it is possible to imagine. Upon the wharf you are assailed by a clamour of English-speaking porters and boatmen. Passing the gates, you come upon a barrack-yard swarming with tall British soldiers, looking wonderfully bright and handsome, after the insignificant figures and soiled, shabby uniforms of the Spanish army. Hence the Waterport Street opens, the principal thoroughfare of the town, though, from its insignificant shops, with English names, and its low public-houses, you have to look up at the strip of bright blue sky above, to be reminded that you are not in an English seaport.

Just outside the principal town, between it and the suburb of Europa, is the truly beautiful Alameda, an immense artificial garden, where endless gravel paths wind through labyrinths of geranium and coronella and banks of flame-coloured ixia, which are all in their full blaze of beauty under the March sun, though the heat causes them to wither and droop before May. During our stay at Gibraltar, it has never ceased to surprise us that this Alameda, the shadiest and pleasantest place open to the public upon the Rock, should be almost deserted; but so it is. Even when the band playing affords an additional attraction, there are not a dozen persons to listen to it; whereas at Rome on such occasions, the Pincio, exceedingly inferior as a public garden, would be crowded to suffocation, and always presents a lively and animated scene.

One succession of gardens occupies the western base of the Rock, and most luxuriant and gigantic are the flowers that bloom in them. Castor-oil plants, daturas, and daphnes, here attain the dignity of timber, while geraniums and heliotropes many years old, are so large as to destroy all the sense of floral proportions which has hitherto existed in your mind. It is a curious characteristic, and typical of Gibraltar, that the mouth of a cannon is frequently found protruding from a thicket of flowers.

The eastern side of the Rock, in great part a perpendicular precipice, is elsewhere left uncultivated, and is wild and striking in the highest degree. Here, beyond the quaint Jewish cemetery of closely set gravestones, bearing Hebrew inscriptions on the open hillside, a rugged path winds through rocks and tangled masses of flowers and palmito, to a curious stalactitic cavern called Martin's Cave. On this side of the cliff a remnant of the famous "apes of Tarshish" is suffered to remain wild and unmolested, though their numbers, always very small, have lately been reduced by the ignorant folly of a young officer, who shot one and wounded nine others, for which he has been very properly impounded.

On the northern side of the Rock are the famous galleries, tunnelled in the face of the precipice, with cannon pointing towards Spain from their embrasures. Through these, or, better, by delightful paths, fringed with palmitos and asphodel, you may reach El Hacho, the signal station, whence the view is truly magnificent over the sea, and the mountain chains of the two continents, and down into the blue abysses beneath the tremendous precipice upon which it is placed.

The greatest drawback to the charms of Gibraltar

has seemed to us to be the difficulty of leaving it. It is a beautiful prison. We came fully intending to ride over the mountain passes by Ronda, but on arriving we heard that the whole of that district was in the hands of the brigands under the famous chief Don Diego, and the Governor positively refused to permit us to go that way. Our lamentations at this have since been cut short by the news of a double murder at the hands of the brigands on the way we wished to have taken, and at the very time we should have taken it. So we must go to Malaga by sea, and wait for the happy combination of a good steamer and calm weather falling on the same day.

IX.

GRANADA.

Hotel de los Siete Suelos, *April* 4.

LATE in the afternoon of the 15th of March we embarked on board the *Liston* in the dockyard of Gibraltar. It had been a lovely day, and the grand Rock had looked its best, its every cleft filled with flowers and foliage. The sun set before we had rounded Europa Point, and the precipitous cliffs of the eastern bay rose utterly black against the yellow sky. Then all was night, and in the warm starlight, the different groups of passengers made themselves comfortable on deck with cushions and mattresses.

At two A.M. a long line of lamps sparkling through the darkness showed that we had reached Malaga; but we had still many hours to wait before the health officers would visit us, without which we were not allowed to land, and daylight gradually broke, and gilded first the mountain tops, and then the massive cathedral, the shipping, and the town. At seven our examiners came, and, standing in a boat beneath the steamer, demanded that all the crew should come up to the side of the vessel. "Show them all your tongues," said the captain, but apparently the inspection was ·not satisfactory, for they came on board afterwards, and examined each separately. Then the passengers were all called out, and great difficulty made because their number was one less than that entered in the books. " Being cannibals, we have eaten him since we left Gibraltar," explained the captain jocosely. At last we were allowed to bestow ourselves and our packages in the fleet of little boats whose owners were fighting to take us to the pier; a tiresome custom-house was ready to prove the Spanish rule that though custom-house duties need not be paid, custom-house officers must—and the proverb, "No hay tan ciegos que los que no quieren ver." Then the watermen, having done their best to extort twenty francs for doing almost nothing, and having, after a battle, been beaten down to ten, at last left us in peace at our hotel.

Malaga is the dearest place in Spain, being the

most Anglicised. The prices there are nearly the double of those in the northern towns. We wondered that it should be so much resorted to by invalids, as, when we were there, a fierce east wind was blowing, and the whole air was clouded with the thin white dust, which is almost a permanent misery, and prevents any enjoyment from walking. There is very little to see. The long Alameda is a dusty walk between insignificant trees, with a very pretty fountain at the end, which was brought by Charles V. from Genoa, and intended for his palace at Granada. The Græco-Roman cathedral was built in the sixteenth century, and is little worth visiting. It occupies the site of a mosque, and stands at the entrance of the moorish quarter of the town, which straggles up one side of a cactus-clothed hill, crowned by the Arabic castle of Gibralfaro. The surrounding country consists of ploughed lands over which the dust-storms sweep uninterruptedly, or yellow hills covered with the productive vines of Malaga.

The journey from Malaga to Granada is a difficult one. The only train leaves at half-past three in the afternoon, and takes passengers to Las Salinas. The railway runs through a gorge of most Salvator Rosa-like scenery, where the Xenil tosses wildly through a great rift in the rocky precipices, sometimes lost altogether beneath the cliffs, and then emerging more boisterous than ever. At Las Salinas two diligences were waiting for us, not nearly enough for the great number of passengers, so the crowding was dreadful. The road from hence was a mere track, broken in some places into deep quagmires and pools of water, mended in others by great lumps of rock thrown loosely down anyhow. Through and over these we floundered, thumped, jolted, and crashed, in a way which was absolutely frightful, especially when a precipice at the side, dimly seen through the night, added to the dangers. Every one was occupied in holding on as they best could. No one had time to think of the robbers, though many were known to be about, and we had an armed escort hanging on behind. As we reached Loja the road improved, and our sixteen mules swung us skilfully round the sharp corners of its narrow streets. In the valley below the town, the railway began again, and in two hours more, at half-past two A.M., we were at Granada, and climbing, in an omnibus, the ascent to the Hotel Siete Suelos, which is within the hallowed precincts of the Alhambra.

There is nothing more interesting than the

awakening in a place new, and yet so old, so well known from stories and pictures of earliest childhood, as Granada. And it was like an awakening in Paradise. Far below our windows a deep green gorge descends towards the town and vega, filled with tall elm-trees and carpeted with violets. Broad, well-kept paths run in different directions through this beautiful wood, skirted by rushing brooks of crystal water. In the different openings of the green glades are lofty stone basins, in which fountains plash and play, not sending forth a narrow jet such as one's recollection of an English fountain conveys, but bursting forth in a foaming mass of abundant waters. Here, nightingales sing incessantly in their season, and the whole wood is always alive with a chorus of singing birds. The trees, the only elms in Spain, except those in the garden of Aranjuez, indeed almost the only trees of any size which are not fruit trees, were planted by the Duke of Wellington. They have never been thinned, and though no individual tree can ever be a fine one, a change can scarcely be wished for, there is such a picturesqueness in the immensely tall, narrow, interlacing stems, in the arching foliage which bends and meets in mid-air over the roadways, and in the swinging garlands of ivy which drop here and there from the high branches. On the right, the red towers of the Alhambra guard the heights; to the left, glimpses of the snowy Sierra-Nevada may be caught here and there through the trees. Almost adjoining the house is the famous tower of the Siete Suelos, from whose postern gate Boabdil, the last of the Moorish kings, passed out with his family after the conquest of Granada. Altogether a more enchanting dwelling-place can scarcely be imagined than the Hotel of Los Siete Suelos.

It is scarcely five minutes' walk through the wood to the entrance of the Alhambra, the grand "Gate of Justice," beneath which the Moorish kings dispensed judgment. Over the first arch is seen a hand with the fingers uplifted as in a Neapolitan talisman. Over the second arch is a key. Only when the hand grasped the key, said the Moors, could the Alhambra be taken. Above the gate runs the inscription placed there by its founder Yusuf, in 1348, "May the Almighty make this a bulwark of protection, and inscribe its erection amongst the imperishable actions of the just." No artist will fail to sketch this gate—either its glowing orange walls, seen through the deep shadows of the wood, or combined with the pictu-

GATE OF JUSTICE, ALHAMBRA

resque Berruguete fountain, of the time of Charles V., which stands beneath its terrace wall.

Hence, by a winding vaulted passage, we arrive at the upper platform of the Alhambra. That part which we reach first, gay with fountains and myrtle-fringed gardens, is called the Plaza de los Algibes—the place of Moorish cisterns. On its left are the rugged range of yellow towers which enclose the Alcazaba-Kassábah, or citadel; on the right is the grand palace of Charles V., built of bright yellow stone, reminding one in its colour of the Coliseum, and in its forms of the Otto Heinrichs Bau at Heidelberg. Its windows, which have never been glazed, frame broad strips of deep blue sky, but its caryatides and bas-reliefs are still fresh as if from the workman's chisel. The arrangement is curious, as the interior is an immense circular court-yard, though the exterior is quadrangular. Beyond the palace are more trees and gardens, a church, a convent, a mosque, a little town, all within the castellated precincts of the hill, which is pointed at both ends, and girdled with towers.

From the terraced wall you look down upon the great town, which is still one of the largest in Spain, though its population, 400,000 under the

Moors, is now reduced to 75,000. Above the vast expanse of whitewashed houses, the churches, towers, and cypresses, rises conspicuously the Græco-Roman cathedral, where the first Christian sovereigns of Granada rest side by side. The nearest hill is covered all over with prickly pear, intersected by narrow paths leading to caves, in which a great part of the gipsy population burrow and live. Between this and the platform on which we stand, rushes the rapid gold-producing Darro, emerging from a rocky gorge in the mountains, and, as it enters the town, becoming lined with the quaintest old houses, leaning, bracketed, over its stream, and looking as if they would topple over every moment. Each wall is full of balconies, upon which bright-coloured clothes are hanging out to dry in the sun, while the parapets are lined with large red vases filled with hyacinths and yellow gladiolus, and pinks and nasturtiums stream downwards luxuriantly from the boxes beneath. Here a high gothic bridge, there a broken Moorish arch, spans the narrow river. As your eye follows the Darro to its junction with the Xenil, the houses become thinner, till at length they are lost altogether in the bright green of the vega, shut in on two sides by chains of beautiful mountains, and backed by the Sierra-Nevada, one sheet of untarnished snow, which, under this deep blue sky, is almost too dazzling to look upon.

If we turn away from the view to the hill-garden itself, what a scene of life and sunshine it is! how fresh its rich foliage and flowers, how abundant its fountains! It is as if all the natural beauties of Spain were concentrated on this one spot, which seems to belong to a different country altogether to the desolated treeless plains of the rest of the peninsula. What picturesque figures are constantly passing backwards and forwards!— copper-coloured gipsies with blue-black hair, the men in embroidered jackets with hanging silver buttons, scarlet fajas round their waists, and broad-brimmed sombreros; the women in bright pink and yellow petticoats, and with large bunches of flowers, generally yellow by way of strongest contrast, pinned behind their black locks. Each scene at the doors of the encircling towers, which are mostly let out to poor families, is a study. What combinations of colour! what picturesqueness in the natural grouping of the figures, with their pigs, their goats, and their dogs, the latter generally called Melampo, Cubilon, or Lubina, because such are said to have been the names of the three favoured animals who accompanied the shepherds to look upon the newly-born Infant at Bethlehem, and dogs called by those names never go mad.

Much of the Moorish palace was destroyed by Charles V. when he erected his own building. That which remains occupies so very small a portion of the Alhambra precincts, and is so concealed behind the later edifice, that at first a stranger will wonder where it can be, and if he goes round to the back, and is told that some low pointed shed-like roofs enclose the most beautiful building in the world, will think it quite impossible. This excessively plain exterior was adopted to avert the evil eye, which scowls upon that which is too prosperous. It is by a narrow alley, ending in a low door-way behind the palace of Charles, that you enter the building. But, as you pass that door-way, you are translated out of fact-land into fairy-land. You never think again about size, all the proportions are so perfect. Court succeeds court, and hall follows hall with a bewildering loveliness of sculpture quite indescribable, and which, though endlessly varied, is perfectly harmonious. A petrified veil of the most delicate lace covers every wall, formed partly by flowers and geometrical patterns, but in the main intention of its fretwork, as strictly religious as the sculpture of a gothic cathedral, and filled with sentences and maxims from the Koran, which it is intended to bring constantly before the eyes and heart of the beholder. Over and over again also occurs the motto " Wa la glaliba—illa—allah," " There is no conqueror but God"— the words which Ibn-l-Ahmar answered to his subjects, when they came forth to meet him as he returned victorious to Granada, greeting him at the same time as " Galib"—the conqueror. The delicate creamy pink of the stucco adds to the magical effect of the whole. The only inmates are the martlets, which build under the overhanging eaves, and are for ever flying in and out of their nests,—the only birds sacred and unmolested in Spain, because they are believed to have plucked off the thorns from the crown of our Saviour as He hung upon the cross. In a few places fragments of colour remain, the primary colours, blue, red, and yellow, having been the only ones used by the Moors in their upper decorations, though the secondary colours, purple, green, and orange, are employed in the Azulejo dados, which are nearer the eye. In the Hall of Justice, where Ferdinand and Isabella heard high mass on taking possession of the Alhambra, are some curious paintings upon leather, nailed to the wooden dome. They represent bearded Moors, sitting cross-legged upon cushions, with their heads covered, and two-edged swords in their hands; and, as the Moors were prohibited from making the exact representation of any living creature, are supposed to have been the work of a Christian captive; others imagine that they were painted after the conquest, and that they only date from the end of the fifteenth century.

The whole Alhambra teems with reminiscences of the romantic history of the two last Moorish sovereigns. King Abu-l-hasan took prisoner the Christian maiden Isabel de Solis, daughter of the governor of Martos, and, falling passionately in love with her, made her his wife under the Moorish title of Zoraya, or "the morning star." The former sultana, Ayeshah, imprisoned in the tower of Comares (so called from its Moorish architect), fearing for the safety of her son Abu-Abdillah, or Boabdil, under the hands of her rival, let him down, with the help of her ladies, from a window overhanging the Darro ravine, and he escaped by night. Thenceforward the palace was filled with dissensions, the powerful clan of the Abencerrages, who were the mainstay of the kingdom, espousing the cause of Zoraya, the Zegris that of Ayeshah. In 1482 Boabdil dethroned his father, and became known as "El Rey Chico." Ayeshah at once urged upon him the importance of conciliating so powerful a family as the Abencerrages, but his spirit of vengeance was too strong, and, inviting the chiefs of the family to a banquet as if to make peace, he had them beheaded one after another in the hall which is called by their name, and where their blood-stains are still shown on the marble pavement. Thirty-three warriors fell thus, and their ghosts may still be heard nightly moaning in the hall where they died. The rest of the family were warned by a page, and forthwith joined the Christian army, under Ferdinand and Isabella, which was already encamped against Granada. In the Hall of the Ambassadors Ayeshah girt her son with a sacred sword, with which he was to repel the invaders. But the young sultana Morayna wept over his departure, when she heard that he had struck his lance against the gateway and broken it—an omen which gave him the name of "El Zogoybi," "the unlucky one."

The city fell January 2, 1492, when Boabdil, having presented the keys and done homage to the Catholic sovereigns, departed for ever by the gate of the Siete Suelos, which, in accordance with his last request to Isabella, was walled up, so that no one might ever use it again. From the spur of the Alpuxarras, still called "El ultimo sospiro del Moro," he looked his last upon the town, and wept as he beheld it. "It is well," said the stern Ayeshah, "that you should weep as a woman for what you could not defend as a man."

Several of the towers round the walls are well worth visiting, especially those of Las Infantas and La Cautiva, which are filled with exquisite Moorish tracery, though much defaced by the French. The latter tower derives its name from a Christian captive who the then Moorish king wished to add to his harem, and who, when she found no other means of protection, flung herself from its window, beneath which her lifeless form was found by her knightly lover, who came that day to her rescue. In the same neighbourhood, in a charming garden, is the beautiful little mosque, in which Yusuf I., the principal builder of the Alhambra, was murdered at his prayers.

Issuing from the walls near this by the Torre del Pico, whose battlements were added by Ferdinand and Isabella, one may cross the glen

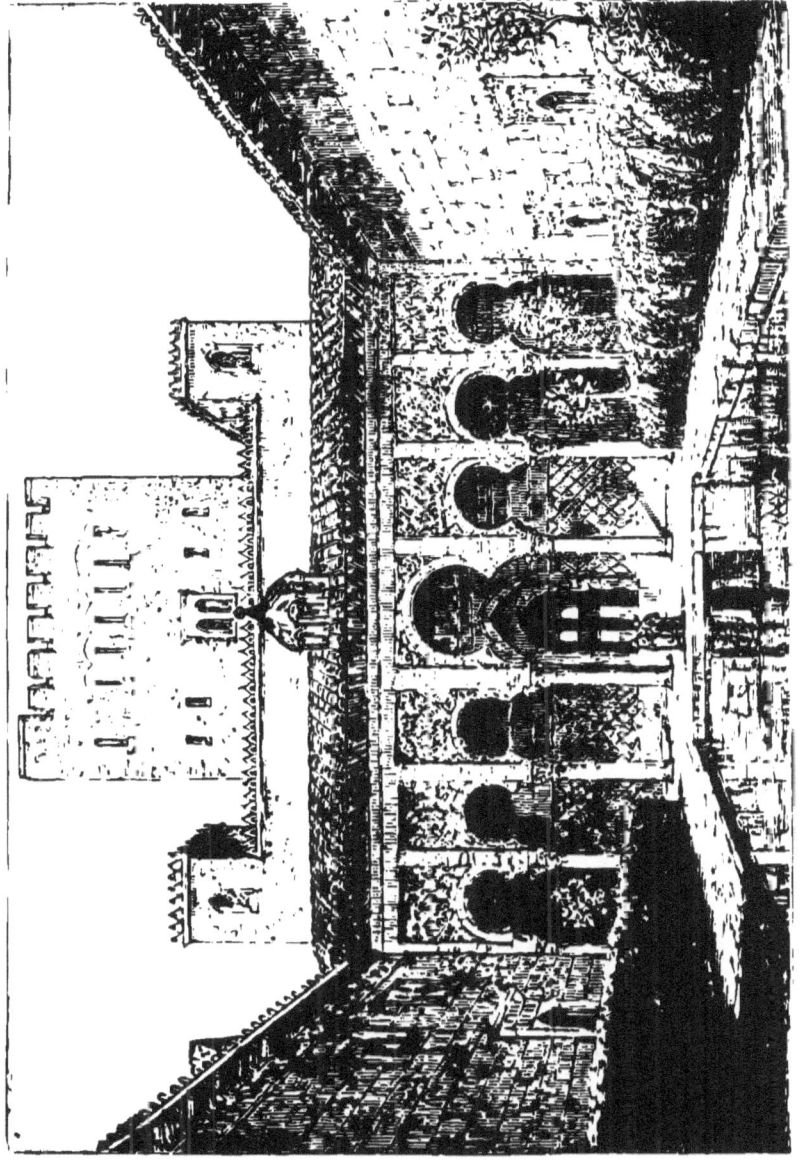

COURT OF BLESSING, ALHAMBRA

to the Generalife,* a summer villa of the Moorish sovereigns. Its gardens are so lovely, with their wide views over the town and vega, that Andersen and many other travellers have even preferred this palace to the Alhambra. Through its cloistered courtyard, rushes, fresh from its source, an impetuous life-diffusing branch of the Darro. Its decorations, much injured by whitewash, are still full of grace and beauty; its faded pictures of the Spanish kings and queens, unimportant as works of art, are yet interesting here from their historic associations; and its venerable cypresses, beneath one of which the Sultana Zoraya is said to have met her Abencerrage lover, are the most magnificent in Spain.

It requires many visits to understand the Alhambra, and for this purpose all who stay any length of time at Granada should arm themselves with an order, " per estudiare," from the governor, Señor Contreras, who lives in the house near the entrance, which contains the beautiful arch called the " Puerta del Vino." Unsupplied with this, the

---

* An order for the Generalife, now belonging to the great Genoese family of Grimaldi, must be obtained in the town from the Italian Consul, who will at the same time exhibit Boabdil's beautiful inlaid sword.

traveller will be incessantly persecuted by the troop of officious and greedy guides who lurk in the entrance. Each light in each hour of the day has its own special charm, and lends its own peculiar effect to some part of the building; but no one should miss a visit by moonlight, when the Court of Lions, strangely expanded in size, looks as if it were wrought in burnished silver, and when all modern changes are lost in shadow, and only the beautiful ideal of the Arabian palace remains in its splendour. At sunset, crossing the kitchen garden which occupies the interior of the Alcazaba, the Torre de la Vela should be ascended for the sake of the view, the last tower on the southern point of the promontory, where, even from Moorish times, a loud bell, beginning at "Las Animas" ($8\frac{1}{2}$ P.M.), and continuing till daylight, has announced to the farmers of the plain that they might turn aside the waters of the river for the irrigation of their meadows. It was upon this tower that the Christian standard and cross were first raised after the conquest, and a cross in the wall still marks the exact spot. Hence the fiery orb of the sun will be seen grandly disappearing behind the purple mountains, and the snowy ranges of the Sierra Nevada bathed with rose-colour in the after-glow. The whole scene will call to mind the lines of George Eliot in the "Spanish Gipsy:"—

> "The old rain-fretted mountains in their robes
> Of shadow-broken grey; the rounded hills
> Reddened with blood of Titans, who huge limbs
> Entombed within, feed full the hardy flesh
> Of cactus green and blue-sworded aloes;
> The cypress soaring black above the lines
> Of white court-walls; the pointed sugar-canes
> Pale-golden with their feathers motionless
> In the warm quiet; all thought-teaching form
> Utters itself in firm unshimmering lines."

While our minds were still full of sympathy for the exiled Moors, and while every detail relating to their conquest was of interest to us, we drove out to Zubia, whither the great Isabella came during the siege, to look upon Granada, and where she narrowly escaped being taken prisoner. After her victory, she erected a hermitage there, to commemorate her escape, which still stands amid some tall cypresses, and contains faded portraits of Ferdinand and Isabella. A thicket of bay is shown as that in which the queen hid herself with her children, and was concealed by the closely entwined branches, like Charles in the oak, until the enemy had passed by.

Another short excursion may be made to Santa Fé, the town which rose during the siege, built in eighty days by the indomitable Isabella, after her troops had been rendered shelterless from the accidental destruction of the camp by fire. Here, the crucifix, which the queen carried with her, is preserved in a small chapel. Not far off is the old bridge of Pinos, the spot which Columbus had reached when, wearied by five years' waiting and petitioning at the Spanish court, he was about to offer his services to Henry VII. of England. Hither the messengers of the queen pursued him, and brought him back to arrange at Santa Fé the expedition which ended in the discovery of America.

The story of the conquest is told in a series of curious bas-reliefs in the "Capilla de los Reyes," which joins the cathedral. Isabella is seen riding into Granada on her white palfrey, with Ferdinand on one side and Cardinal Mendoza on the other, Boabdil presents the keys, and numbers of despondent Moors are pouring out of the gates of the town. Again, the Moors are represented as being baptized *en masse*, their costume exactly the same as that which may still be seen at Tangiers. In front of the retablo which contains these sculptures, are the magnificent tombs of the Catholic sovereigns. Ferdinand and Isabella lie side by side upon a lofty sarcophagus. Both figures are beautiful, but that of Isabella (Elizabetha in Latin) is indeed worthy of her whom Shakespeare called "the queen of earthly queens," and Lord Bacon describes as "an honour to her sex and the corner-stone of the greatness of Spain." The effect of her character upon those she lived amongst, is touchingly portrayed in a letter written by Peter Martyr from beside her death-bed:—"You ask me of the state of the queen's health. We all sit in the palace all day sorrowing, and tremblingly await the hour when religion and virtue shall quit the earth with her. Let us pray that we may be permitted to follow whither she is now going. She so far exceeds all human excellence, that there is scarcely anything mortal left in her. Hers can hardly be called death, it is rather the passing into a nobler and higher existence, which should excite our envy instead of our sorrow. She leaves a world filled with her renown, and goes to enjoy a life everlasting with her God in heaven. I write in the alternations of hope and fear, while her breath is still fluttering within her."

Close to that of her parents, is the tomb (a beautiful work of the Genoese Peralta) of Joanna and her handsome husband Philip of Burgundy. In the vault beneath, the four coffins may be seen. That of Philip is most interesting, as being the same which Joanna carried about with her everywhere, often passionately embracing it, and watching it constantly for forty-seven years, in the tearless madness of her long widowhood. A magnificent reja by Bartolomé of Jaen (1533) screens off the tombs from the rest of the chapel. Round the cornice is inscribed:—" This chapel was founded by the most catholic Don Fernando and Doña Isabel, King and Queen of Las Espanas, Naples, Sicily, and Jerusalem, who conquered this kingdom and restored it to our faith; who acquired the Canary Isles and the Indies, as well as the cities of Oran, Tripoli, and Bugia; who crushed heresy, expelled the Moors and Jews from these realms, and reformed religion. The Queen died Tuesday, Nov. 26, 1504. The King died Jan. 23, 1516. The building was completed in 1517." In the sacristy are portraits of Philip and Joanna, and in one of the chapels of the cathedral are fine pictures of Ferdinand and Isabella, copies of the originals by Rincon, which were destroyed by fire.

The plan of the cathedral (which is the work of

Diego de Siloe, son of the sculptor of the tombs at Miraflores) is a very noble and peculiar one. The central aisle, forty feet in width, instead of ending in an apse, expands into a dome seventy feet in diameter, beneath which is the high altar. The side aisles also end in altars; an ambulatory surrounds the whole. In the side chapels are very fine works of Alonzo Cano, especially one of that picturesque subject often treated by Spanish painters—"the Solitude of the Virgin."

There is a great deal more to be seen in Granada. The principal Moorish street, "El Zacatin," remains, and, adjoining it, the "Alcaiceria," or silk bazaar, consisting of two narrow alleys, beautifully adorned with stucco and sculpture in the style of the Alhambra. Of the same character is the old Moorish gateway on the other side of the Darro, built in 1070, but now called "Puerta del Carbon," from the Carboneros who frequent it. Near the Darro, opposite the ruin of a horse-shoe bridge, is a Moorish bath, having a coved roof supported on low pillars, with richly carved capitals. The church of San Geronimo was built in 1497 by Talavera, confessor of the Catholic sovereigns, and first Archbishop of Granada. He was anxious to convert the Moors by kindness, and translated the church services into Arabic for their use. He afterwards wished to translate the Bible likewise, but was prevented by Cardinal Ximenes, who declared that "Hebrew, Greek, and Latin were the only languages in which the word of God ought to be used—the three languages plainly pointed out to mankind by the inscription on the cross itself." San Geronimo contains the empty tomb of the great Captain Fernando Gonsalez of Cordova, who lived at Granada during the latter years of his life, being driven to a life of complete retirement by the jealousy of Ferdinand and the animosity of his second queen Germaine. At the very time of his death Ferdinand had given orders for his arrest, fearing that he was about to embark for Flanders, yet the king and the whole court went into mourning for him, and a hundred banners waved above his tomb till the year 1600. His painted statue remains in the church, with that of his wife Doña Maria Manrique, who survived him only a few days, but their bodies are no longer here; they were actually exhumed by the revolutionary Government in 1870, and carried in a tin box to Madrid, where a kind of Pantheon has been made in the church of San Francisco el Grande with labelled pigeon-holes for all the great men of

Spain. Some English travellers, wishing to take seats in the diligence that day, were told that they could not have them, because the places were bespoken for El Gran Capitan!

The neighbouring hospital of San Juan de Dios is very interesting, as having been founded by the saint himself in the early part of the sixteenth century. He preached the necessity of hospitals on this spot with such ardour that he was considered mad and shut up in an iron cage, which is shown. His teaching, however, still brings forth fruit here, and the hospital, whose wards all open upon a spacious cloistered quadrangle, is admirably arranged and attended to.

Hence a short walk into the country brings one to a spot bearing the Moorish name of Hinadamar, where stands the Cartuja, a Carthusian convent and church, decorated somewhat in the style of the Certosa of Pavia. The jaspers, marbles, and inlaid work of ebony and tortoiseshell are very gorgeous, though their taste may be questioned. The most real treasure preserved here is a small statuette of San Bruno by Alonzo Cano, one of the most expressive representations of touching humility and suffering that can be imagined. The old guide delights to point out the quaint images formed by the vagaries of the veins in the alabaster and agate decorations—an "Ecce Homo," a "Mater Dolorosa," a "Grenadina in her Mantilla," &c. The cloisters are surrounded by a horrible series of paintings, representing the history of the order, especially the awful sufferings of the English Carthusians under Thomas Cromwell, which, if true, may weigh heavily in the scale against the martyrdoms under Catholic Mary. These pictures are the work of Juan Sanchez Cotan, a brother of the order, who was of such eminent piety and purity of life, that the Virgin herself is believed to have descended from heaven in order to give him a sitting for her likeness, upon which he was engaged.

As he returns to the town the pedestrian should pause, for here, at the entrance of Granada, occurred one of the most striking scenes of history. The body of the beautiful and beloved Isabella of Portugal, wife of Charles V., had been brought hither by slow stages, attended by all the young knights who had faithfully served her in life. Among these was Francis Borgia, Duke of Gandia. At the entrance of Granada the corpse was uncovered, and the attendants pressed forward to gaze upon the honoured features of their mistress for the last time. But under the terrible hand of death all her beauty had disappeared, and Borgia was so overwhelmed by the change of decay, that he abandoned for ever the vanities of the world to become an ascetic, a priest, and eventually a saint of the Catholic Church.

Wearied by much sight-seeing, a tourist may refresh his eyes and mind in the beautiful Alameda near the junction of the Xenil and Darro, where the aristocratic part of the population, always conscientiously employed in doing nothing, unite every summer evening and winter afternoon. The ladies universally wear mantillas and carry fans; the gentlemen are so well dressed that Mr. Poole himself might take a lesson from the crack tailor of Granada. The older Alameda, lined with fine old trees, and ending in fountains, is not inappropriately called "El Salon," for there society meets and does its chief business. It is a regular evening party in public and in the open air, a Vanity Fair in miniature,—the unmarried daughters, followed by their admirers, being paraded up and down by their parents, not unmindful perhaps of the old Spanish proverb, "Three daughters and a mother are four devils for a father." On festas the assembly extends to all classes, and numbers of majas may be seen in gaudy dresses with flowers in their hair, attended by their majos in their velvet jackets and bright sashes, and with the stick—"vara"—in their hands, without which no well-bred majo ever appears in public. More, probably, is spent upon dress, taking all the classes together, in Spain than in any other country of Europe; only, in the provinces, the soldiers often appear shabby and ragged, for they are not only irregularly paid, but are sometimes unsupplied with even the most necessary articles of clothing. Thus the following placard appeared upon the walls of the Andalusian towns proposing a reward for the defenders of Algeciras and Tarifa:—"El brigadier Cordoba ha abierto una suscricion, poniendose á la cabeza de ella, para regalar un *par de pantalones* de paño à los valientes soldados de Asturias."

In the week preceding Passion Week large placards appeared, headed by a picture of the Crucifixion, and the words, "Jesu Redemptor" in large letters. They announced a "Passion Play" to be acted in the theatre. The whole story of the last days of our Saviour was enacted, as at Ober-Ammergau—the Last Supper, and the Crucifixion itself, being represented upon the stage. A burlesque was by no means intended, yet some parts bordered upon the ludicrous. One scene was rapturously encored by the audience; it was when Judas descended to the infernal regions amid a crash of thunder and a blaze of blue lights! It is due to the venerable Archbishop of Granada to say that he strongly deprecated this exhibition, and did all he could to oppose it.

All the ceremonies of Holy Week at Rome are reproduced on a minor scale here, and on Holy Thursday the Archbishop washes the feet of twelve pilgrims in the cathedral. On Good Friday the whole population wear black.

Easter Sunday is a great day in Granada, not because the resurrection of our Saviour is commemorated on that day, but because then at five P.M. the famous "Virgen de las Angustias" goes forth from her church to visit a sister-image in the cathedral. That afternoon the streets assumed the most festal appearance; the windows were hung with red, yellow, and blue draperies, and the balconies were filled with gaily dressed ladies. Long before the hour arrived the whole of the Alameda was filled from end to end with a dense multitude of expectant people, and hundreds of boys were rushing about in front of the sanctuary waving long branches of green elder, which they threw down under the feet of the bearers as they carried the image down the steps of the church; literally they "cut down branches from the trees and strewed them in the way." This image of the Virgin of Sorrows is one of the most famous in the south of Spain, and half the women in Granada are christened Angustia, to place them under her protection; indeed the name is so common as to cause inextricable confusion amongst the number of Angustias. The figure is of the size of life, and is better as a work of art than most worshipped images of saints. It is dressed in black velvet robes spangled with golden stars, wears a crown on its head filled with precious stones, and has a sad, pensive expression in its countenance, which is bent over the dead figure of the Saviour—for it is, in fact, a Pietà. Its jewels are most magnificent, and such is the enthusiasm and courage it is known to inspire, that when the French came to Granada they never ventured to plunder or even enter this church, though the people, in defiance, had decorated the Virgin with all her jewels, lighted the church by night and day, and left the doors always open.

As the image left the church, carried by the principal citizens of Granada in full dress, a blare of trumpets and crash of drums greeted its appearance. Guns were fired, and rockets sent up; the noise was deafening. As the procession entered the Alameda, with one impulse the whole people fell upon their knees. Many women wept and sobbed as they stretched out their hands in eager supplication. At each step of the procession fresh fireworks rose from the houses on either side of the way; it was like a march of fire, and the appearance of the tall black figure slowly advancing up the green avenue between the throng of kneeling people, was certainly most striking.

A very different scene was enacted upon the evening of Holy Thursday, when, in an upper chamber, seventy earnest Protestant converts met to receive the sacrament of the Lord's Supper at the hands of a Protestant Presbyterian minister. The liturgy used was almost entirely that of the English Prayer-Book, which is translated into Spanish. The elements were received seated, according to the Presbyterian custom. In spite of the power of the Virgin of Las Angustias, Protestantism is making strong advances in the town where Matamoros suffered. Nothing has a greater effect upon the Spaniards than our Burial Service; its reverence, its encouragement of Christian hope, contrasting so strongly with the indecent indifference with which the Romanist funerals of the lower classes are conducted at Granada, where no ceremony whatever takes place at the cemetery, and where the bodies, carried unattended to the grave, are buried like dogs, generally ejected from their coffins (which are used again!), and with only a little earth scraped over them. The hollow way between the red towers of the Alhambra and the green slopes of the Generalife, torn by a torrent, and filled with hundreds of pigs which are herded there, is called "The Way of the Dead," because by that rough path the bodies are generally carried from the town to the cemetery. We witnessed several of these saddest of funerals. Once it was a beautiful little girl who was to be buried. She was borne upon an open bier, her waxen features, smiling in the sleep of death, were crowned with white roses and jessamine, her little hands were folded, she was dressed in white, and other white flowers were sprinkled over her. All had evidently been done by the tender care of loving friends. Yet no one followed but the grave-digger smoking a cigar, and the little bier was jerked jauntily along by six rough boys of thirteen or fourteen years old, some of whom were smoking, the rest whistling and singing. We could hardly bear to think of the fate which awaited that little child at the cemetery, where, when these uncoffined funerals take place, the gipsies, by an ancient custom, fall upon the body on its arrival, and tearing off all its dress and decorations, fight and scramble for them amongst themselves, leaving the poor corpse to be tossed, naked and desecrated, into its grave amongst the docks and nettles.

The savage insolence of the gipsy population, their coarse language and manners, and their brutal immoralities, are the great objection to a lengthened residence in Granada. They are absolutely uncontrolled either by the laws or the police. Their swarms of children are brought up systematically to beg without ceasing, and to steal whenever they can. They are utterly without shame. If an English lady ventures into the gipsy quarter alone, a troop of young women and children will not scruple to fall upon her, and while some carry off her shawl, parasol, &c., others will force their hands into her pockets and seize all it contains. Gipsy beggars never ask, they always demand, in the most violent and imperious tones, and wherever a number of gipsy children are encountered together, the shouts of "ochavito, ochavito," are more than deafening. Unfortunately the view from San Nicolao, one of the grandest in Granada, is in a stronghold of the gipsies, who must be encountered to visit it. Their chief residence, however, is in the hillside of the Albaycin, leading to the Monte Sacro, where innumerable caves are perforated in the living rock, beneath immense prickly pears, which serve at once as food, shade, and protection. The mouths of these caves are whitewashed, and the entrances generally guarded by a piece of old carpet. There the savage families bask all day in the sun, and make the air resound with their harsh guttural cries and songs. The women who do not steal, earn money by telling fortunes and selling amulets; the children who are not busy begging, roll in the dust in front of their caves, often quite naked, and without any distinction of sex.

It is impossible not to be struck by the originality and cleverness of the gipsies even in their vices. A gipsy-man was at confession one day, and, whilst he was confessing, he spied in the pocket of the monk's habit a silver snuff-box, and stole it. "Father," he said, immediately, "I accuse myself of having stolen a silver snuff-box." "Then, my son, you must certainly restore it." "Will you have it yourself, my Father?" "I, certainly not," answered the confessor. "The fact is," proceeded the gipsy, "that I have offered it to its owner, and he has refused it." "Then you can keep it with a good conscience," answered the Father.

At Seville a stranger, wishing to see the manners and customs of the gipsies, may, on paying one real ($2\frac{1}{2}d.$), be present where they dance their national dances and sing their national songs in their own picturesque costume. At Granada a few women in tawdry white muslin gowns extort five francs from every individual of the large assemblies who have the folly to meet to see them. Their principal dances are the Malagena and the Romalis. A woman generally dances alone at first, in slow motion, more with her arms than her feet, and her attitudes are often very picturesque and graceful. Gradually, by her gestures, she invites a partner to join her; thenceforth the dance becomes more animated. They chase one another, they circle round one another, they throw a whole story of passionate eloquence into their gestures, and all is accompanied, in the way of music, by the clapping of hands of all the other gitanos and gitanas sitting round in a circle, who keep excellent time together, occasionally bursting into loud outcries, which reach a pitch almost of frenzy when any especially complicated figure is successfully executed.

For the last few days of March it was very wet and stormy. They say it is always so in Spain, and concerning this there is an old Spanish story. A shepherd once said to March that if he would behave well he would make him a present of a lamb. March promised to deserve it, and conducted himself admirably. When he was going out, he asked the shepherd for the promised lamb, but the sheep and the lambs were so very beautiful, that the shepherd, considering that only three days of restraint remained to March, answered that he would not give it to him. "You will not give it to me," said March, "then you do not recollect that in the three days which remain to me, and three which my comrade April will lend me, your sheep will have to bring forth their young;" and for six days the rain and cold was so terrible that all the sheep and all the lambs died.

With the beginning of April, we were persuaded, by glowing accounts of its scenery, to make from Granada the long excursion to Llanjaron, a mountain citadel, the last stronghold of the Moors in Spain. But the distance is so great and the long diligence journey so fatiguing, that this expedition is not worth while, except in summer, for the sake of ascending the Veleta, one of the highest peaks of the Sierra-Nevada. The road runs along the high bleak uplands beneath the chain of the Alpuxarras, which are by no means the rich, verdant, smiling hills they are generally represented, but volcanic, bare, and arid in the highest degree. The name Alpuxarras is an Arabic word, meaning "Land of Warriors." Amid these fastnesses, according to the ballad, fell the famous Christian knight Alonzo de Aguilar, as he was endeavouring to accept the challenge of Ferdinand to his bravest warriors that they should plant his banner on the highest peaks of the mountains:—

> " Qual de vosotros, amigos,
> Ira à la Sierra mañana,
> A poner mi real pendon
> Encima de la Alpuxarra."

Here Alonzo's brave boy Don Pedro de Cordova fought by his side covered with wounds, and refused to attend to his entreaty—"Let not the hopes of our house be crushed at one blow; go live as a Christian knight, go comfort your desolate mother"—till he was forcibly carried out of the battle by the attendants.

We reached Llanjaron by a terrible road along precipices and through torrent-beds, but it is an oasis in a hideous desert, and its orange gardens, hanging on the edge of the mountain-side over a dismal ravine, are amongst the most productive in Spain. On a high outlying spur of the hills is a ruined Moorish castle; but the village, chiefly frequented for the sake of its medicinal waters, contains few traces of its former occupants; the population is savage, the posadas miserable, and beyond bread, eggs, and oranges, there is no food to be had.

X.

ARANJUEZ AND TOLEDO.

IT is almost a blur upon the entire pleasure of a visit to Granada, that all arrivals and departures by train are necessarily in the middle of the night, and that the hotels are consequently in a chronic state of disturbance from one to four in the morning. Even though we decided upon taking the diligence to evade the long railway détour by Cordova, we had to leave at four A.M., when our last drive to the town through the dark woods of the Alhambra seemed a solemn farewell to one of the most beautiful places upon earth.

In a whirlwind of white dust, ten horses carried us quickly along through a sterile, treeless, hideous country. At one P.M. the scenery improved a little, and the great white cathedral of Jaen rose before us at the foot of its jagged mountains. The diligence waited for an hour in the market-place, which gave time for its driver and mayoral to dine, and for us to see the inside of the cathedral, a Græco-Romano building of 1532, but very handsome of its kind. Behind the Coro is a silver Custodia with seven keys, only opened three times in the year, and containing one of the many pieces of linen, honoured by the Roman Catholic Church as the *authentic* handkerchief with which Santa Veronica wiped the face of our Saviour on His way to Calvary, and upon which His image remained impressed. This especial relic, however, is of historic interest, as having been carried by St. Ferdinand at the head of his troops.

At four in the afternoon we reached the quiet station of Mengibar, a lonely shed on a bank above the Guadalquiver, seeming a strange termination for a long diligence journey, but a very convenient spot for joining the train from Cordova to Madrid. We passed our waiting time in a tea-garden, surrounded by a hedge of oleanders, which grow wild in profusion all over this neighbourhood.

Before daybreak we had reached Aranjuez, and were walking across its white dusty squares and through the long corridors of its deserted palace, something like a very miniature Versailles, to the pleasant little quiet hotel of Los Infantes, which may be strongly recommended to travellers as both clean and economical. The host, too, is a pleasant kindly person, who, in the evening, sate in his open wooden gallery, playing on his guitar, with his men and maid-servants singing around him, in happy patriarchal fashion. It is desirable to know of this resting-place, because the Hotel de Paris at Aranjuez is one of the worst man-traps in Spain; and an English lady with her two servants, lately captured to wait there between two trains, found themselves locked in till they had consented to pay 230 reals for their luncheon and waiting-room. Another place to be avoided is the wretched and only posada at Mengibar, which extorts fifteen francs for a single egg. Such thieves are rare in Spain, but there is no redress from them.

We spent a day in seeing the sights of Aranjuez, which is the first place where we have been persuaded to take one of the guides, who are generally the greatest bane of a traveller's comfort, but who are, perhaps, desirable here, as saving time where many silver keys and permessos are required. For, strangely enough, in this place, which the railway renders almost a suburb of Madrid, and where the miles upon miles of parks and gardens would be most grateful to its parched citizens, as well as to the residents of Aranjuez itself, the government, though the present court never visits the place, is sufficiently careless of popularity to keep everything closely shut up; so that gardens, such as at Carlsruhe or Stutgard form the delight of the whole population, are here entirely unused except by the thrushes and nightingales.

The larger of the two palaces, a rambling French château, is little worth seeing, except for china-fanciers, who will be delighted with a wonderful room entirely walled and ceiled with beautiful Capo di Monte. This was one of the extravaganzas of Charles III., who did not scruple to waste £3,000 of gold by mixing it with the brass rails of a back staircase in his other Aranjuez palace. This, which is most inappropriately called the Casa del Labrador (the Workman's Cottage), is about a mile distant from the town. Its rooms, though low, are most gorgeously fitted up with exquisite silk embroidery and hangings. Both palaces are filled with reminiscences of curious court scandals and crimes, but especially those connected with Charles III., Maria Louisa, and her lover Godoy, the Prince of Peace, whose position was so easily accepted by the dissolute court, that his being represented, with the king, in a fresco which still remains in one of the principal rooms, was no matter for offence. The extraordinary trio had a passion for clocks, and no less than forty-eight clocks adorn their small apartments in the Casa del Labrador, five or six in each room. All the royal residences of Spain are decorated in this way. The mania which Ferdinand VII. had for clocks is amply shown in the palace at Madrid, and even Charles V. made a collection of them, and remarked how absurd it was to try to make two men's heads think the same, when he could not make two of his clocks go alike.

Aranjuez is an oasis in the wilderness. The Tagus and Xarama, meeting almost beneath the palace walls, keep its island garden fresh and verdant, even through a burning Spanish summer. The fine old English oaks and elms were brought over by Philip II., and were, perhaps, the only good which accrued to his native land from his marriage with our Mary. They still attract as much notice in Spain as a wood of palms and prickly-pears would do at Hampton Court. The beauties of Aranjuez have been a constant theme with the poets of Castile: Calderon and Garcilasso have written in their praise, and even Fray Juan de Tolosa, the Augustine prior of Zaragoza, when he published a religious treatise in 1589 for the benefit of the young knights of the period, called it "The Aranjuez of the Soul," in order the better to entice them to read it. The gardens remain as we see them portrayed in the faithful pictures of Velazquez in the Museo at Madrid, and as they are described by Lady Fanshaw, English ambassadress in Spain during the reign of Philip IV. Long shady avenues of elms and plane-trees lead through closely-planted woods, and have been the scene of countless intrigues, both of politics and love. Even down to the late revolution, all old customs of the place were kept up, even to the breed of camels, introduced here by Philip II., to perform the garden work, and their oriental forms, slowly parading through the shady groves, were a well-known characteristic of the place. Isabella II. never failed to spend the spring months at Aranjuez, but now it is the picture of desolation; fountains without water, beds without flowers, promenades without people: truly one may say with Schiller, "Die schönen Tage in Aranjuez sind nun zu ende."

A short journey by rail, and a long wait in the

wretched junction station of Castillejo—where the only accommodation is a miserable room, open at both ends, and a prey to beggars and dirt of every description—brought us to imperial Toledo. At a distance the town rises grandly, not distinguished by any one marked feature or building, except its great Alcazar, which is chiefly of the last century, but an irregular line of towers, battlemented walls, and ancient houses, crowning the black precipitous rocks, which rise abruptly from the yellow Tagus, and backed by rugged hills, scorched and parched into every shade of orange and brown by the tropical sunshine. The general views of Toledo have no beauty, but are solemn and affecting beyond those of all other places, so huge and historical does it stand, without any vegetation whatever, girdled in from the living world by the indescribable solitude of its utterly desolate hills.

Guarding the entrance of the town stands the ruined castle of Cervantes, on a projecting spur of the mountain. At its foot is the bridge of Alcantara, "the Bridge of the Bridge," closed at both ends by gate towers, and striding with high arches across the Tagus, as it rushes through the deep chasm in the rock upon which it is built.

Hence one ascends to the town by a terraced road, from which there is a glorious view over the Vega. The atmosphere is so clear that every fissure in the distant hills can be counted, and each building on the line of the horizon stands out against the transparent turquoise sky as if seen through a microscope. Where the terrace makes a zigzag to a higher level, is the grand Moorish gateway called Puerta del Sol, richly embossed with tracery, and of a splendid orange-red colour. Now we reach the Zocodover, a Moorish square overhung by many ranges of balconies, whence a tolerably wide street, the only one in Toledo, winds along the irregularities of the hill to the cathedral, which unfortunately stands so low that its fine spire can never become a conspicuous feature. Diving thus into the heart of the town, the quaintness of everything is increasingly striking. Here a beautiful Moorish or Gothic fragment breaking the line of white-washed walls, there balconies adorned with clustering vines and jessamine, hung with bird-cages, and with handsome dark-eyed women in lace mantillas, leaning over their railings. Near the cathedral, at 16, Calle Santa Isabel, is a house of this kind—the pleasant Casa de Huespedes (board-

PUERTA DEL SOL, TOLEDO.

ing-house) of the three excellent sisters Figuerroa —where we spent five days very comfortably. Our sitting-room had the pleasantest of balconies, filled with birds, and common but luxuriant flowers, and looked across a quiet little garden, with a tree—a valuable possession in Spain—to the cliffs on the other side of the river.

Of course our first visit was to the cathedral, and our first sensation was certainly one of disappointment, but perhaps partly because we had heard so much, and expected so much, and because the beggars are so tiresome, and their perpetual whine, with their mischievous, even malicious, tricks, such a constant irritant to the temper. Much also of the building has been whitewashed, and the fact is commemorated in a triumphant inscription on one of its walls!

Still, the beauties of the cathedral of Toledo are such as grow upon one at each sight of it, and surely no church interior was ever more entirely picturesque than this, where the coro, filled with wonderful carved stall-work, divided by jasper pillars, breaks, but does not block, the view of the five naves and their eighty-eight columns, through which the ancient glass sparkles with colours of sapphire, ruby, and emerald, and where the painted and gilt retablo, toned but uninjured by age, rises from pavement to ceiling in an indescribable labyrinth of niches, statues, and sculptured tracery. Around the altar are glorious tombs of some of the earlier kings, Alonzo VII., Sancho del Deseado, Sancho el Bravo, and the Infante Don Pedro. Here also is buried Cardinal Mendoza (ob. 1495), who obtained the name of Tertius Rex, from the degree in which he shared the sovereignty with Ferdinand and Isabella.

Behind the high altar, in a large chapel of their own, are magnificent tombs of a knight and a lady. He is Alvaro de Luna, Master of Santiago, Constable of Castile, and Prime Minister of John II., whose mind and counsels he completely ruled for five-and-thirty years. He lived with royal state, and when he rode out was followed by thirty knights, and he held three thousand lances in his pay. His interference brought about a marriage between his king and Isabella of Portugal, who became his bitterest enemy, and whose ascendancy over her husband was the cause of his ruin. He was executed on an accusation of high treason in the square at Valladolid, his last words being, "And this is the reward of faithful devoted service to my king." In his lifetime he had prepared beautiful bronze tombs for himself and his wife, but when he was disgraced his relentless master had them broken up, and they were made into the two pulpits which still stand at the entrance of the Capilla Mayor. The existing tombs, of alabaster, are due to the filial piety of his daughter Maria.

Close by is the entrance of the Capilla de los Reyes Nueves, built by order of Juan II., and containing a statue of its founder (buried at Miraflores), and the tombs of Henrique II. (1379), and his queen Juana (1380); their son Juan I. (1390), with his wife Leonora (1382); Henrique III. (1407), and his wife Catalina de Lancastre (1419), daughter of John of Gaunt.

The Sacristia Mayor, entered near this, is surrounded by beautiful pictures of Juan de Borgoña, in the style of Perugino. Below these hang a most interesting series of authentic portraits of the archbishops. They include Mendoza and Ximenes, by Borgoña; Carranza, the confessor of Charles V., who urged the dying emperor to faith in the Crucified as the only Saviour, and was consequently imprisoned—as "infected with Lutheran opinions"—for eleven years in the castle of St. Angelo, where he died in a dungeon; and

Sandoval (by Luiz Tristan), who urged Philip IV. to the expulsion of the Moors from Spain.

At the western end of the church is a Gothic tabernacle with a beautiful relief of San Ildefonso receiving a chasuble from the Virgin, who is supposed to have presented it in person as he was praying on this spot. An inscription formerly attested the miracle in these words :—

> "Quando la Reina del cielo
> Pusó los pies en el suelo
> En esta piedra los pusó
> De besarla tened uso
> Para mas vuestro consuelo."

The Virgin is also said to have attended mass in this cathedral, occupying the seat of San Ildefonso (never used since) who had written a treatise in defence of her perpetual virginity; and it is to this story of an honour paid to one of its archbishops that Toledo owes the primacy of Spain.

The image which now occupies the place of honour in the shrine, so delighted the Virgin when she came to inspect the likeness, that she declared it her very image, embraced it tenderly, and conferred upon it the gift of miracles. Yet, after all, this is not the most important idol in the place. "Maestra Señora de Toledo," herself one of the most hideous of all the black dolls poor St. Luke is held responsible for, resides in the Sacristy, and possesses a wardrobe and collection of jewels of unparalleled richness. When we saw her, she was dressed in silver tissue, entirely covered with small pearls; but her clothes are changed at each great feast-day.

No one should leave the cathedral without visiting the Mosarabic chapel, a large separate building entered near the great western door. Its history is this. At the Moorish invasion, the Toledans defended themselves gallantly, and, when they yielded, obtained the best conditions they could. Chief amongst the terms they insisted upon was that they should preserve five churches, in which there should be free liberty of worship for those who remained faithful to Christianity. Thus, through the four hundred years of the Moorish rule, the faith was kept alive in Toledo, and the faithful bore the name of Mos-Arabes— "mixed with the Arabs." In the reign of Alonzo VI., when Toledo returned to the Christian rule, the papal legate, Richard, desired that the Mosarabic should be laid aside for the Gregorian ritual, and his wishes were upheld by the king, and the queen Doña Costanza, who preferred the rites of Rome. The Toledan clergy were furious, and the people became so excited, that a revolution was imminent. Alarmed at this turn of affairs, and fearing to push matters to an extremity, the king then proposed as a compromise, after the fashion of the day, that the dispute should be decided by a single combat, each party choosing a champion, and that so God should show which ritual was most acceptable to Him. The fight took place in the vega, and the Mosarabic champion, Don Ruiz de la Matanza, was the victor. The populace rent the air with their applause, and believed that all was settled. But the court was enraged, and some little time after, Alonzo, conveniently discovering that the means of proof chosen had been impious and cruel, proposed another trial. This time, after a general fast, and prayers in all the churches, copies of the Roman and of the Toledan rituals were to be placed together in a lighted bonfire, and that which remained unscathed would be the one approved by God.

A pile of faggots was lighted in the Zocodover, in the presence of an immense concourse, and the two breviaries were placed upon it, each party praying fervently for the liturgy they preferred.

But it was a stormy day, and before the flames could reach it, the Roman prayer-book was taken up by the wind and blown intact and unsinged out of the fire, while the Mosarabic breviary remained unconsumed in the midst of the flames. Both parties shouted that the victory was theirs, but the Mosarabians carried the day, and their liturgy, described by Dr. Neale as "the connecting link of the eastern and western rites," was preserved in Toledo. When Ximenes became archbishop, it was beginning to fall into desuetude, and to preserve so interesting a relic of faith in troublous times, he instituted, in 1512, an order of priests especially charged with the performance of the Mosarabic office, and built the chapel which we see. Its walls are covered with frescoes by Juan de Borgoña, of victories over the infidels, and of the taking of Oran.

The splendid collection of church vestments is well worth examining. Nothing can describe their magnificence, or the degree of high-art to which they shew that needlework can be carried.

The grand time to visit the cathedral is the festival of Corpus, when the whole of its exterior is hung with glorious tapestries of the time of Ferdinand and Isabella.

The existing remains in Toledo are of three kinds, viz., first, the Moorish mosque, the Moorish houses, and the fragments of Moorish work embedded in the cathedral and churches; second, the Jewish synagogues; third, the Christian art.

The Moorish mosque, now called the church of El Christo de la Luz, is of intense interest. It stands behind the Puerta del Sol, and might easily be overlooked, as its walls, covered with beautiful Moorish arches, are enclosed in a courtyard. It was in existence when Alonzo VI. entered Toledo, May 25, 1083. Built into this and other Arabian buildings of Toledo are fragments of Gothic constructions, such as capitals and portions of columns, showing that they belonged to Christian edifices anterior to the Moorish conquest. The plan adopted by the Moors is almost analogous to that of the Christian basilicas, their mosques being divided into naves, and generally ending in an apse. The arches which support the roof of the naves are either round or horseshoe, and double arches are employed in the ornamentation of the walls. The shafts of the columns which sustain the arcades of these buildings are either of marble or of brick and mortar, but always thick and heavy. The octagonal form observed in some of them is a feature of the period. The arabesques and carvings with which the Moors ornamented their work in Toledo are almost always coarse adaptations from the ornaments which they had seen in passing through places which had submitted to their yoke. Their capitals follow the Greek forms, more or less modified, according to the caprice of the builders, but Byzantine ornament is the kind which was most popular with them.

There is something especially striking in the low vaulted nave of El Christo de la Luz, which is like a miniature fragment from the mosque at Cordova. Over the altar hangs a ghastly crucifix with long real hair, which recalls a curious Spanish legend, telling that as the Cid rode by after the conquest at the head of his troops, his faithful steed Bavieca dropped upon its knees before this mosque. Bavieca needed no guidance and never did wrong, so when she knelt all knew that some holy relic must be concealed upon that spot. The wall was pulled down, and, as the stones fell, a stream of light poured forth, and a crucifix was disclosed, where it had been immured for safety before the invasion, the lamp which was then lighted still miraculously burning—El Christo de la Luz.

Near this church is the splendid hospital of

Santa Cruz, now a military school. Cardinal Mendoza left his fortune to Isabella to be employed for charitable purposes, and this is one of the noble foundations she raised in fulfilment of what she felt would be his wishes. Its patios and staircase are as beautiful in detail as in design.

Quite on the other side of the town are the two marvellous old Jewish synagogues, now called El Transito and Santa Maria Blanca. Both are of the greatest interest, as having been built by the Jews during the dominion of the Moors, under whose tolerant rule they enjoyed perfect freedom and liberty of conscience. Both buildings are almost like mosques, and it is supposed that Moorish workmen were employed in them. Santa Maria Blanca, which stands back in a little court, and is newly whitewashed, was indeed a Jewish sanctuary, being ceiled with cedar of Lebanon, and the ground on which it stood covered with the sacred dust of Palestine.

El Transito is much more magnificent. It was built by Samuel Levi, a Jew who was the treasurer and faithful servant of Pedro the Cruel, but whose master, coveting his wealth, tortured him and put him to death, and then confiscated all his possessions.

When the Christians recovered Toledo, the star of the Jews set, and each Jewish head was taxed at thirty pieces of silver—" the price of Him whom they of the children of Israel did value." But they were allowed to retain their synagogues through a curious plea. The Jews of Toledo affirmed that they had not consented to the death of the Saviour! When Jesus Christ was brought to judgment, they said, the council of Jews, of which Caiaphas was the president, sent to take the votes of the tribes as to whether He should be released or put to death. One tribe voted for his acquittal, and from them the Jews of Toledo were descended. This tribe, then, was guiltless of the blood of Jesus, and did not merit the execrations poured upon their brethren. The original answer of the Toledan Jews, with a Latin translation of the Hebrew text, is preserved in the archives of the Vatican.

In 1389 the oppression of the Jews began by their being bereaved of their market, which was near the cathedral, by Archbishop Tenorio, who built the present cloister on its site. In 1454 Santa Maria Blanca was taken away from the Jews, on the instigation of San Vicente Ferrer. This saint was a great mixture. Cruel and vindictive beyond words in his persecution of heretics, he was saint-like in the practice of his own life. He refused all Church dignities; daily he read and meditated upon the Scriptures, especially upon the Passion of our Lord. In his treatise on the "Spiritual Life," he exhorted men to turn to God constantly in prayer, for "study would drain the heart and intellect unless men constantly turned to place themselves at the foot of the cross of Christ, when the thought of his sacred wounds would give fresh power and new light to their souls."

In 1490, the Toledans, in order to have a plea for a further spoliation of the Jews, gave out that they had stolen Juan Passamonte, a boy of Guardia, and crucified him, putting his heart into a hostia, as a charm against the Inquisition. This story is commemorated in a fresco near the beautiful cloister gate called "El Niño Perdido," and is, like the similar story of St. Hugh of Lincoln, a favourite theme with poets and painters. In 1492 every unbaptized Jew was forced to quit Spain by Ferdinand and Isabella, and 170,000 were cruelly expelled, preferring banishment and the loss of everything to abandoning their faith. The expulsion of the Jews was the ruin of Toledo. It is strange how, throughout these persecutions, the teaching of St. Bernard was overlooked, who said, "Take heed what you do to the Jews, for whosoever touches them is like one who touches the apple of the eye of Jesus, for they are His flesh and blood."

Not far from the synagogues is the church of San Tomé, containing a picture by the rare artist El Greco (Domenico Theotocupuli — 1577-1625). It represents the burial of the Conde de Orgaz, in 1392, by St. Stephen and St. Augustine, who are believed to have come in person to bury him, because he had spent all his wealth in adorning their churches. Near this, almost on the edge of the steep cliff which overhangs the Tagus, is the Franciscan convent of San Juan de los Reyes, with its beautiful church, built by Ferdinand and Isabella in memory of their victory at Toro. It will at once attract attention, not only from its Gothic architecture, but from its being hung all over with the links of the chains of Christian captives rescued at the conquest of the Moors. The entrance, built by Alonzo de Covarrubias for Philip II., is surmounted by an exquisitely-sculptured cross. The cloisters, though of late Gothic, are amongst the most beautiful in Europe. Latterly nature has added much to their charm, and jessamine and honeysuckle form natural crowns around its saint-statues. Here Cardinal Ximenes entered upon his noviciate as a Franciscan monk, and hoped to flee from the world in which he was destined to play so conspicuous a part.

Close to the church are the Cyclopean ruins of the palace built by King Wamba in 674, and inhabited by Roderick. From its window he is said to have beheld the beautiful daughter of Count Julian, who had been intrusted to his care, while she was bathing in the river, and to have become possessed with the fatal passion which led to the invasion of the Moors, and the destruction of his kingdom.

In the hollow is the grand gate-defended bridge of San Martino, connected with which is a curious anecdote of wifely devotion. The architect of the original bridge on this site discovered too late that his work was not strong enough, and would give way when the scaffolds were removed. To his wife alone he communicated his misery; she set fire to the scaffolds, burnt down the whole work, and saved her husband's reputation.

Beyond the bridge the river leaves its rocky gorge and winds through the plain. Here is the small ancient basilica called El Christo de la Vega, with its richly-decorated apse and solemn Rembrandt-like interior, in which the principal ray of light falls upon the figure on the crucifix which gives a name to the sanctuary. The figure, which is of life size, has its head bent, its hair falling over the shoulders, one hand only nailed to the cross, and the other extended as if in the act of taking an oath. Its story tells that a young country girl made her lover promise to marry her and sign a paper swearing that he would do so before this crucifix,—that afterwards the lover was faithless and denied his troth, when the maiden, deserted and weeping, betook herself to the chapel, and prayed, and laid the paper he had signed before the altar, imploring help from her Redeemer; — then, in the solemn stillness, the Crucified detached one hand from the cross, and stretching it out, exclaimed, "Io soy testigo,"—I am the witness!

A recent Spanish author, Gustavo Becquer, says truly: "Outside the place which guards their memory, far from the precincts which preserve their traces, and where it appears as if we still breathed the atmosphere of old tales told in the evening, traditions lose their poetic mystery, their inexplicable hold upon the soul. Far off one questions, one analises, one doubts; but here, faith, like a secret revelation, illuminates the spirit, and makes one believe."

Good walkers should ascend, to the left, beyond the bridge of St. Martino. Passing the rude stone cross on the edge of the hill, they will find themselves at once in one of the wildest scenes imaginable, and may follow a path which winds through a gorge, and then along declivities so arid that scarcely anything grows there except asphodel and cistus, flowers which are careless about water and love a dry sandy soil. Rosemary too flourishes in the clefts, a herb which Spanish peasants think it impossible to estimate too highly. Once, they say, it was a poor common plant of the field, but upon it the Virgin, on a washing-day, hung out to dry the baby-clothes of the infant Jesus, and thenceforth it became for ever green and fragrant and full of virtues. The fact is commemorated in one of the popular songs, which are so endless in themselves, and so endlessly in the mouths of the people as they work :—

> "Lavando estaba la Virgen,
> Y tendiendo en el romero;
> Los parajitos cantaban;
> Adoremus el misterio."

Since the death of the Saviour, too, it is believed that the rosemary has put forth fresh flowers every Friday, the day of his suffering, " as if to embalm his holy body."

As the path winds higher amongst the rocks, we come in sight of a hermitage and its little chapel of the Virgin. Hither, on the night of her great festival on the 1st of May, long processions toil up, chanting as they go, and all the little ways are lit up by blazing branches, making a winding path of fire in the darkness. Beyond the chapel is the ghastly and desolate gorge called the Degollada, from a woman who had her throat cut there, and truly it seems a fitting place for such a deed, which might easily be concealed here; and as the environs of Toledo are a stronghold of brigands, it requires something of an effort to mount the last and most desolate ascent which ends at the Castle of Cervantes. Yet no views give one such an idea of the solemn desolation of Toledo as these, whence the tawny river is seen winding for miles between jagged cliffs, crowned on the other side with buildings so weird, so uniformly old, and so hopelessly decayed, that it is impossible to believe that one is still walking in the nineteenth century. So, in spite of brigands, it is well to linger here till sunset, when all the poor and pitiful detail is lost, and only the stupendous outline remains, engraven upon a flaming sky. "Then," to quote Becquer again, "the lofty and black needles of the towers of Toledo, between whose arched windows fall some last rays of light, stand out against the floating groups of golden clouds, like a legion of phantoms, who, from the height of their seven hills, look down upon the plain with their eyes of fire."

In the valley beyond the bridge of Alcantara is another ruin, called the "Palace of Galiana." This legendary princess is supposed to have been the daughter of King Golafre, who loved her passionately and built her a palace, compared with which all the glories of the Arabian Nights paled into insignificance. Hither endless lovers came courting, and annoyed the princess dreadfully, but the most hideous and wearisome was Bradamant, a gigantic Moorish chieftain, who made an underground passage from his stronghold at Guadalajara to Toledo, that he might visit her every day. At length Charlemagne the Great came hither to assist Golafre against Abderrhaman, the Sultan of Cordova, and being lodged in the palace and falling in love with Galiana, he slew Bradamant and presented her with his head.

The princess was so charmed with the gift that she became enamoured of the giver, accepted his hand, accompanied him to France, and was crowned triumphantly. Such is the legend. The palace, which never was a palace, and which certainly never was inhabited by Galiana, is reduced to a few crumbling walls. Near it, in strange contrast, runs the railway, and it is the last building seen on leaving Toledo.

XI.

MADRID AND THE ESCORIAL.

IT is because Charles V. suffered so much from the gout, that Madrid was chosen as the capital of Spain. He found relief from its sharp air, and it was thenceforth adopted as the home of royalty. No situation can possibly be more odious to ordinary mortals. Though situated 2,400 feet above the sea, it has none of the advantages and all the disadvantages of a high position. The climate is burningly hot in summer and piercingly cold in winter.

> "El aire de Madrid e tan sotil
> Que mata a un hombre, y no apaga a un candil."*

All around, the country is utterly barren and hideous. Not a tree, not a drop of water, not a green plant,

* "The air of Madrid is so subtle. It kills a man, and does not put out a candle."

not even a blade of grass, not a vestige of colour of any kind, but only roads deep in dust, and a district covered with brown sand, or dull grey rock. After the time of Philip II., the kings of Spain found out how great a mistake had led to the desertion of the old royal cities of Valladolid, Toledo, Seville, and Granada for this desert, and Philip III. wished to move back the capital to Valladolid, Charles III. to Seville, but it was then too late, partly because the building of the Escorial had added such a heavy link to the chain which bound the capital to Madrid—which is neither a "ciudad," nor a cathedral-town, but "the largest village in Spain."

> "Quien te quiere, no te sabe;
> Quien te sabe, no te quiere,"*

is a very true proverb regarding the present royal city, yet the self-glorious Spaniards still call theirs "the only court," and believe that the world is silent in awe before its splendour.

> "Donde esta Madrid calle el mundo?"

and another proverb says that it is but one step from Madrid to heaven :—

> "Desde Madrid al cielo."

---

* "He who wishes for you, does not know you;
He who knows you, does not wish for you."

There was a small town on this site before the time of Charles V., and its narrow streets are interesting and abound in historical recollections. The Plaza San Domingo marks the site of a conventual church where Pedro the Cruel was buried, and his tomb, removed when the church was pulled down, may be seen in the architectural museum. In the tower of the Casa de Lujanes and in the adjoining house which has a curious doorway, Francis I. was imprisoned. The house called Las Vistillas was that where Ferdinand and Isabella resided when at Madrid, and from its balcony Cardinal Ximenes answered the nobles who demanded by what authority he had assumed the regency, by shewing them his soldiers in the court beneath. The Plaza Mayor, still antiquated and picturesque, was the scene of many Autos da Fé. "Many Jews are burnt here," wrote Madame de Villars, ambassadress in the reign of Charles II., to Madame de Coulanges, "and there are other tortures for heretics and atheists, which are horrible to think of." The Court looked down upon these scenes from the windows of a house still remaining, and worth visiting on account of its fine staircase lined with rich blue azulejos. From these windows also Charles I. of England saw a bull-fight, given in his honour by Philip IV., when he was courting the Infanta Maria. At that time there was no regular Plaza de Toros, and bull-fights were always given here, and were the cause of far greater loss of human life than those which exist at present, as the greater proportion of the bull-fighters were not professional, but young noblemen of the court, who hoped to make themselves more acceptable by exhibiting wild feats of rash daring under the eyes of their mistresses. Vivid descriptions of these bull-fights are given in the exceedingly rare but important letters of the Comtesse d'Aulnois, a French lady of rank, who visited the court of Spain during the reign of Philip IV. "The Plaza Mayor," says Madame d'Aulnois, "is larger, I think, than the Place Royale at Paris. It is rather long than wide, surrounded by porticoes, upon which the houses are built, and are always alike, five stories high, with a range of balconies in each, upon which you enter by large glass doors. The balcony of the king stands more forward than the others, is larger, and covered with gilding. It occupies the centre of one side, and is surmounted by a canopy. Opposite are the balconies of the ambassadors, the Councils of Castile and Arragon, the Inquisition, Italy, Flanders, and the Indies. The offices of War, the Crusades, and Finance are to the right of the king; one may recognise them by the arms which are displayed on their crimson velvet hangings, embroidered with gold. Lastly, the town council, the judges, the *grands*, and other nobles, are placed according to their rank, and at the expense of the king, or of the town, who hire the balconies from different private persons who live there.

"There is given on behalf of the king, to all those I have mentioned, a collation in appropriate baskets, and with this collation, which consists of fruits, sweetmeats, and iced-waters,—gloves, ribbons, fans, pastils, silk stockings, and garters are offered to the ladies; so that these festivals always cost more than a hundred thousand crowns, an expense which is defrayed from the fines appropriated to the king or to the town. This is a fund which no one would venture to touch, even to save the kingdom from the greatest danger; if they did so, a sedition would be the result: so great is the delight which the people take in pleasures of this kind.

"I assure you, that the countless crowd of people (for every place is filled, the roofs of the houses like the rest), the balconies with their gay hangings, the number of beautiful ladies, the magnificent Court, the guards, and in short, the whole square, present one of the most beautiful sights I have ever seen.

* * * * * *

"When there are in the town horses which have served and are skilful in a bull-fight, even without any knowledge of their owner, they are borrowed from him, equally if he does not wish to sell them, or if there are no means to buy them with, and they are never refused. If the horse is unfortunately killed, and a proposal is made to pay for it, it is not allowed, and it would be shewing a want of Spanish generosity to receive money in such a case. It is nevertheless sufficiently disagreeable to have a horse, which you may have taken great pains to bring up, and which any adventurer may kill in the most unconcerned way. This kind of combat is considered so perilous, that indulgences are open in many of the churches on those days, on account of the slaughter which takes place. Many Popes have wished entirely to do away with such barbarous spectacles, but the Spaniards have been so urgent with the court of Rome to leave them untouched, that it has given in to their wishes, and up to this time they have been tolerated.

* * * * * *

"The fêtes are beautiful, great, and magnificent; it is a very noble and costly spectacle; it is impossible to depict them fairly, and one cannot imagine them without seeing them. But I confess that all this gives me no pleasure, when I think that a man whose safety may be dear to you, has the rashness to expose himself to a furious bull, and that for love of you (for this is generally the motive), you may see him return bleeding and half-dead. Can one approve any of these customs? And suppose even that one has no special interest in them, can one wish to be present at these fêtes, which nearly always cost the lives of many persons? For my part I am astonished that in a kingdom, whose kings bear the name of Catholic, such a barbarous amusement should be allowed. I know it is of great antiquity, as it dates from the Moors, but it seems to me that it ought to be quite abolished, as well as many other customs derived from these Infidels.

* * * * * *

"A cavalier of merit was in love with a fair young girl, who was only a jeweller's daughter;

but she was perfectly beautiful and a great heiress. This young nobleman having learnt that some of the fiercest bulls of the mountains had been taken, and thinking that he would derive great honour from their conquest, resolved to fight with them, and asked his mistress's permission. She, horrified at the very idea of such a proposition, fainted away, and forbade him, using the whole force of her influence over him to prevent his risking his life. In spite of this prohibition, he thought he could not give her a higher proof of his love, and secretly prepared everything which he required. But notwithstanding the care which he took to conceal his design from his mistress, she discovered it, and left no stone unturned to change his resolution. At last the day of the fête arrived, and he conjured her to be there; assuring her that her very presence would be sufficient to make him a conqueror, and to acquire for him a glory which would render him more worthy of her. 'Your love,' she said to him, 'is more ambitious than tender, and mine is more tender than ambitious. Go where glory calls you. You wish that I should be present, you wish to fight before me; yes, I will accede to your wish, and perhaps my presence will cause you more trouble than encouragement.'

"At last he quitted her, and went to the Plaza Mayor, where all the world was already assembled. But he had scarcely begun to defend himself against a fierce bull that had attacked him, when a young peasant threw a dart at the terrible beast, which pierced it, causing great agony. It instantly left the young nobleman who was engaged with it, and rushed bellowing against the person who had struck it. The young man aghast tried to escape, when the cap which covered his head fell off, and the most beautiful long hair in the world floated over his shoulders, and revealed that it was a girl of sixteen. So petrified was she with terror, that she was unable either to run or escape the bull, which gave her a terrible wound in the side, at the very moment when her lover, who was the *tocador*, and who recognised her, came to her assistance. O God! what was his anguish, at seeing his dear mistress in this terrible state! He became beside himself, life was valueless to him, and more frantic than the bull itself, he performed incredible feats. He was mortally wounded in several places . . . That was indeed a day when people considered the fête delightful."

The Plaza Mayor, now no longer used for bull-fights, is occupied by an open garden, through

STATUE OF PHILIP IV., MADRID.

which, in pleasant contrast to London squares, people are allowed to circulate freely. In its centre is the grand equestrian statue of Philip III., cast by John of Bologna from a drawing by Pantoja. A still grander statue is that of Philip IV., where the bronze mane and scarf literally float on the air, and which is historically interesting from the important persons employed in its design; Velazquez supplied the drawings, it was cast in Florence by Pedro Tacca, and Galileo shewed how the great weight of the horse could be sustained in its prancing position. This statue, moved from the gardens of the Buen Retiro, now ornaments the centre of the Plaza del Oriente, one side of which is occupied by the palace. This is certainly one of the most magnificent royal residences in the world, imposing in itself, and striking from its position at the end of the finest part of the town, on the edge of a steep bank. The nearer detail of the surroundings is wretched, rugged slopes and ragged shrubberies, walks and gardens alike hopelessly neglected, but, beyond these, it looks upon the snow-capped range of the icy Guadarrama. Below, in the hollow, dribbles the Manzanares, which can scarcely be called a river, and which has been compared by

Tirso de Molina to that dreariest of things, a university town during the long vacation.

> "Como Alcalá y Salamanca,
> Teneis y no sois Colegio,
> Vacaciones en Verano
> Y curso solo en Invierno."

In the reign of Charles II., the Court used to amuse themselves by driving up and down in the dry bed of the river, and Madame de Villars gives Madame de Coulanges an amusing account of the scenes which took place there. She also mentions, apropos of the enormous bridge which there crosses nothing at all, that a wit of the time suggested to Philip IV., that he had better buy a river, or sell his bridge.

The royal family of Spain of the house of Austria, of which we read so much in memoirs of the period, which was such a strange chaos of beauty and ugliness both mental and physical, need not remain even personally strangers to any one. In the Royal Gallery, where many delightful and profitable mornings may be spent, Titian, Pantojo, Coello, and Velazquez, have handed down to us their living forms so vividly that we may still walk and live amongst them. The family procession begins with Charles V., first standing with his favourite dog; again, as an old man, with a grizzled beard, upon his war-horse. Here also (hung too high) is the portrait of his beautiful queen Isabella of Portugal, which he carried with him to San Yuste; and near it is Titian's strange picture of the Apotheosis of Charles V. and Philip II., in which they, kings on earth, kneel as suppliants before the throne of the Redeemer. This was the last object which met the dying eyes of the Emperor; and, by his own desire, was long hung over his grave. In connection with his portraits we should look at those of his daughter, Juana of Austria, who, as widow of a Prince of Portugal, was Regent of Spain during the absence of Philip II. in England; of Catherine, Queen of Portugal, sister of the Emperor; and of Mary of Portugal, the unnatural daughter of his other sister, Queen Eleanor.

Philip II. is portrayed for us, in several distinct stages of his life; and it is most interesting to trace from youth to age the progress of the handsome features that never smiled except when he heard of the massacre of St. Bartholomew, when he laughed outright. Three of his four wives may be seen with him; Mary of Portugal, Mary of England, and Isabella of France, the daughter of Catherine de Medicis. The grand portrait of the ugly Mary

Tudor, by Antonio More, is especially valuable, as being that sent over to shew her bridegroom what she was like before their marriage, and it is wonderful that, after gazing upon her sour features, he should have decisively thrown over a charming princess of Portugal to marry her. Near the queen, is the portrait of Antonio Perez, the cruelly persecuted minister of Philip II. Then come his children, —Don Carlos, whose birth cost the first Mary her life, and whose own sad life is supposed to have been closed by his father's cruelty; and Clara Eugenia Isabella, the beautiful daughter of his third wife, whom her father spoke of as his "mirror" and "the light of his soul," and to whom he bequeathed the Netherlands. Then Philip III. and his wife Isabella ride by on their magnificent horses. Then begin the endless portraits of Philip IV., with those of his first wife Isabella, daughter of Henry IV. of France, and their little son Balthazar, who died before he was grown up, represented with a gun at six years old, and again riding splendidly on his little pony; of the minister Duke of Olivares; of Don Ferdinand of Austria, the king's handsome brother, with his beautiful dog; of the second Queen Mariana, who never could help laughing, in spite of the stiff solemnity of the Spanish court, and who looks as if she must herself have provoked laughter by her extraordinary coiffure and costume as a bride; of her little daughter Maria Margherita, a charming child, in the most enormous of hooped petticoats, repeated again and again, at prayers, in full costume, and playing with "Las Meninas," her maids of honour, while her father and mother, looking in at the door, are reflected in the opposite mirror. Here also is Charles II., the last lineal descendant of Charles V., and his charming wife Marie Louise d'Orleans, of whom he was so enamoured, that he exclaimed on seeing her dance, "My queen, my queen, thou art the most perfect in all creation."

Upon the other treasures of the Madrid gallery it is impossible to dwell here. They cannot be studied enough, from the rich colouring of Raphael, Titian, and Pordenone, to the cold skies and almost too truth-telling figures of Velazquez. Never was there a more delightful collection, though there never was one worse arranged, or in which it is more difficult, almost impossible, to find what you want.

The interest in the royal portraits must be carried on to the Armeria at the other side of the town, where, in a great hall, stand, as if marshalled in battle array, a grand troop of suits of armour, which include many of those in which the kings were painted. Perhaps the most interesting armour here is the suit worn by Isabella at the siege of Granada; the most interesting individual specimen, the weird Norse-like helmet of Jaime el Conquistador. Charles V. is again brought home to us in his camp bed, and his portantina, brought from San Yuste. In the suits of armour which belonged to him, the figure of the Virgin is always engraved upon the breast, that of St. Barbara, his patron saint, upon the back.

In the Academia are preserved three splendid Murillos taken from the Caridad at Seville by the French, and never sent back there when Waterloo restored them to Spain. The finest represents St. Elizabeth of Hungary (Santa Isabel in Spanish) caring for her lepers, the others tell the story of the fall of snow which led to the foundation of Sta. Maria Maggiore at Rome. Here also may be studied the extraordinary pictures of Goya (ob. 1828) king's painter to Charles IV., and justly called the Rabelais of painting; they are wonderful representations of Spanish life, or of wild dreams of witchcraft, effected by scratches, plunges, lunges of pen and pencil, with dabs, splashes, and blots of colour.

Modern Madrid has deserted the gardens of the Buen Retiro, in which the Austrian court so delighted, and goes to amuse itself on the promenade of El Prado, which is something like the Champs Elyseés, though a bad imitation. Here, the dusty road between the avenues is rendered supportable by perfect volumes of water being squirted over it, and the trees are enabled to grow by having little ponds dug round their stems. It is quite worth while to go here late in the afternoon. The costumes of the nurses are really gorgeous, brilliant scarlet, orange, and purple, slashed with broad stripes of black velvet, and forming perfect rays of colour as they dart in and out after their children under the acacia trees. Here groups sit on the stone seats discussing the last pictures in *La Carcajada*, a capital newspaper of political caricatures; and young legislators of from eighteen to twenty, got up excessively smart, consider that they are the only power which has a right to direct the affairs of the world. At the gay little wooden stalls all varieties of cooling drinks—" Bebidas "—are sold, the prince of which is " Horchata de Chufas," a kind of snow-milk flavoured with the juice of a little nut which comes from Valencia. " Confituras " are also sold here—

a great favourite being that known as "Cabello de Angel," or "Angel's Hair." Picturesque groups of peasants gather around these stalls, not Mayos and Mayas here, but "Manolos" and "Manolás," a corruption from Manuel and Manuela. Up and down, between the passers-by, flit the water-carriers, and make the air resound with their sharp cry of "agua, agua, quien quiere agua ; agua helado, fresquita como la nieve."

The upper end of the Prado is lined on one side by little gardens. This is the aristocratic part of the promenade, where society must always go *de rigueur* as far as a certain fountain, and where "the language of fans" is talked to an amazing extent. Descending the other way, one comes to Atocha, a monastery with a church, raised into a basilica by the present Pope to please Queen Isabella and Don Francesco d'Assis. These "Catholic sovereigns" always came once a week to worship a hideous idol-Madonna (another of poor St. Luke's); and on March 22, 1854, solemnly decorated it with the collar of the Golden Fleece. For centuries the image had been celebrated. In 1562, when the whole kingdom was in suspense during the alarming illness of Don Carlos, heir of Philip II., it was carried to his sick-room at

Alcala, and shares the honour of his cure with the dead body of the monk Fray Diego, which was dug up and laid upon his bed. Ferdinand VII. came hither especially to invoke the assistance of the Virgin of Atocha, when he conspired against his father; and, when he was carried off by the French, he transferred the ribbon of the Immaculate Conception to its breast from his own. To this church also came the Italian king Amadeo, straight from the station, to look upon the dead face of the murdered Prim.

The other churches of Madrid are all modern and little worth seeing. San Isidro Real, however, may be visited, as containing the relics of the ploughman's saint, invoked in wet weather by the peasant, in the popular couplet—

> "San Isidro Labrador
> Quita el agua y pon el sol."

San Isidro was a common labourer who neglected his work to make meditations upon the virtues of San Isidoro, which is supposed to have been considered so meritorious above, that angels were sent down to do his work for him, and wolves were unable to devour his oxen. He died in 993, and was canonised because Philip III. was cured of some trifling illness upon touching his body. When Queen Isabel came to pray by it, one of her maids of honour, pretending to kiss his toes, bit one of them off, feeling sure that her health would be benefited by swallowing so great a relic; but she instantly became dumb, and did not recover her speech till she was able to vomit forth the delicious morsel. The festa of San Isidro is greatly observed on May 25th, at Madrid, and the pilgrimage on that day to San Isidro del Campo is a very pretty sight. But, on the whole, saint-worship has been on the wane here for some years past, and Protestantism making great ground. Large shops full of Bibles are no uncommon sight now in the streets of Madrid, and have a great sale. It is interesting to remember that when the first Spanish translation of the Bible was made in Spain by Francisco de Enzinas in 1543, Charles V. did not oppose it, and even promised to accept its dedication to himself, if only the Church would approve it. The Church, however, was furious, and it was condemned to be burnt, and its author was cast into prison.

For the last few years "society," in the generally accepted sense, has almost ceased to exist at Madrid, having been so divided by political estrangements. Don Carlos has many friends, the Prince of Asturias ten times as many, "the inoffensive Italian," as the aristocratic Spaniards contemptuously but pityingly call him, scarcely any; indeed, the Italian queen, Vittoria, has only found two ladies willing to take office in her court. Many rules of ancient etiquette are preserved which are curious. Everything in Madrid counts by nine days. For instance, after a death in a family, the Novenário must take place : the widow and daughters, or whoever the nearest surviving relations may be, are expected to hold the *Duélo*, that is, to close their windows, and remain solemnly seated for nine days in their reception rooms to receive the condolence of all their friends, who visit them in mourning; and as it is the correct thing for all the friends to repeat their visit during every one of the nine days, though the first two or three times they are all very solemn and sad, it is impossible to keep up the strain, and the party naturally glide into a degree of gossip and chatter which is a desecration alike of the occasion and of the feelings of those who have to go through the ordeal. Widows, however, may be thankful to escape all they had to go through at Madrid in the last century, when they were compelled to pass the whole first year of their mourning in a chamber entirely hung with black, where not a single ray of the sun could penetrate, seated on a little mattress with their legs always crossed. When this year was over, they retired to pass the second year in a chamber hung with grey. They could have neither pictures, nor mirrors, nor cabinets, nor any ornamental furniture, during the whole of their widowhood. They were never allowed to wear jewels, and still less, colours. However modest they might be, they must live so retired that "it seemed as if their souls were already in the other world;" and, according to a writer of the time, this great constraint was partly occasioned "because some ladies who were very rich and especially in beautiful furniture, were often induced to take another husband, in order to have the pleasure of using it again!"

In the Royal Gallery, poor Mariana, wife of Philip IV., the laughing queen, whom we have seen tricked out in all her bridal bravery, is introduced to us for a second time in her widow's dress. It consists of thick black stuff, with a tunic of fine muslin made like a surplice, descending below the knees and following all the lines of the figure. The head and throat are covered with a coif of white muslin, concealing all the hair like the dress of a nun. Over all is a great mantle of black taffetas falling to the feet.

A visit to Madrid finds its natural close in the Escorial, where the kings and queens of whom we have seen so much, have found a ghastly sepulchre. It is so profoundly curious that it must of necessity be visited, though it is so utterly dreary and so hopelessly fatiguing a sight, that it requires the utmost Christian patience to endure it. Well may Théophile Gautier exclaim, that whatever the other ills and trials of life may be, one may console oneself by thinking that one might be at the Escorial, and that one is not.

The Escorial may be undergone upon the road northwards, or may form a separate excursion from Madrid. The station of the name lands you at the foot of the hill on which this colossus of granite is placed. It is generally described as standing in a mountain wilderness, but this is not quite true. You ascend through woods which are pleasant enough, and where Charles IV., wisely declining to inhabit the "architectural nightmare," built a pretty little toy palace of his own. But behind the Escorial all is a bleak solitude, blue black peaks, capped with snow, and furrowed by dry torrent-beds, or sandy deserts sprinkled over with boulders of granite. There is no softening feature. The dismal streets of granite houses which surround the huge granite palace and church have the same lines of narrow prison-like windows, the same harsh angular forms everywhere. The main edifice was thirty-one years in building, and is three quarters of a mile round, but each wall is just like the other, they have no distinguishing features whatever. It has thirty-six courts, and eleven thousand windows, in compliment to the virgins of St. Ursula, but they are all the same size, and all exactly alike. The architect, Herrera, was tied down to the most hideous of plans, that of a gridiron, because it was the emblem of St. Laurence, upon whose day, the 10th of August, the building was vowed after the successful siege of St. Quentin. The whole is justly looked upon as a stone image of the mind of its founder, Philip II. And the interest which encircles this cruel yet religious, this superstitious yet brave, character, lends a charm even to the Escorial. Except the extirpation of heretics, it was the one object of his earthly ambition. The seat is shewn—*Silla del Rey*—high among the grey boulders of the hillside, whence he used to watch the progress of the huge fantastic plan, as court after court was added, each fresh wing forming another bar of the gridiron. When it was finished, he deserted his capital, and made it his principal residence, devoting himself to an eternal penance of fasting and flagellation, but at the same time boasting that he governed two worlds from the heights of his mountain solitude. Hither, when he felt the approach of death, during an absence at Madrid, he insisted upon being brought, borne for six days in a litter upon men's shoulders, and here, during his last hours, he was carried round all the halls, to take a final survey of the work of his life.

The main entrance is so featureless as almost to pass unnoticed. It leads into a vast gloomy courtyard, at the end of which are huge statues of the kings of Judah. These decorate the façade of the church. Its interior is bare and dismal, but the proportions are magnificent, and though the effect is cold and oppressive, it is not without a certain solemnity of its own. In high open chapels on either side of the altar, kneel two groups of figures in gilt robes. On the left are Charles V., his queen, his daughter, and his two sisters; on the right are Philip II., three of his wives (the unloved Mary of England being omitted), and Don

Carlos. Down a long flight of steps you are led by torchlight to the *Panteon*, an octagonal chamber surrounded by twenty-six sepulchres of kings or mothers of kings, arranged one above another like berths in a ship. Charles V. occupies a place in the upper story. Brantôme declares that the Inquisition proposed that his body should be burnt for having given ear to heretical opinions. It remains, though curiosity, not heresy, has twice caused the coffin to be opened; the last time in 1871, during the visit of the Emperor of Brazil, when hundreds of people flocked forth from Madrid to look upon the awful face of the mighty dead, which was entire even to the hair and eyebrows, though perfectly black. Philip II. fills the niche below, lying in the coffin of gilt bronze which he ordered to be brought to him that he might inspect it in his last moments, and for which he ordered a white satin lining and a larger supply of gilt nails, with his last breath. Each of the Austrian kings seems to have loved to pass hours here in meditation over his future resting-place. Philip IV. used to sit in his niche in his lifetime to hear mass; Maria Louisa scratched her name upon her future urn with a pair of scissors. The last funeral here was that of Ferdinand VII., whose coffin was too big for the royal hearse, and had to be brought hither in a common *coche de colleras*, its end projecting from the front windows, the attendant monks riding round it on mules, and the empty hearse following, for the sake of decency. His widow, Christina, though the mother of a sovereign, will never be buried here, even if the Bourbons return to power, as Spanish aristocratic feeling would not allow the honour to a queen who has formed a mésalliance in her second marriage. Isabella II. heard midnight mass in the Panteon whenever she visited the Escorial.

A separate chamber has the dreadful name of *El Pudridero*. Here lie sixty members of the royal family, including Don Carlos, Don John of Austria, and the many queens-consort who were not mothers of kings.

Through the bare cold passages of the convent one may reach the Coro, which contains a celebrated crucifix by Benvenuto Cellini. The stall is still shown which Philip II. occupied, and where he was kneeling when the messenger arrived breathless with eager haste from Don John of Austria to announce the victory of Lepanto, but could obtain no audience till the monarch had finished his devotions. From hence it is but a few steps to the low bare rooms which the bigot king occupied as a dwelling. They are full of interest. The furniture is the same, the pictures, the table, the chairs, the high stool to support his gouty leg. At the bureau which still exists he was sitting writing when Don Christoval de Moura came in to announce the total destruction of the Spanish Armada, the scheme on which he had wasted a hundred million ducats and eighteen years of his life. Not a muscle of his face moved. He only said, "I thank God for having given me the means of bearing such a loss without embarrassment, and power to fit out another fleet of equal size. A stream can afford to waste some water, when its source is not dried up."

The inner room opens into the church by a shutter. At this opening the ghastly figure of the king was seen present at the public mass during his illness, following the prayers with an agonized fervour of devotion. Here also he sate on the morning of the 13th of September, 1598, and, having summoned his children, Philip and Clara Eugenia Isabella (so well known to us from their pictures) to embrace him, received extreme unction, and, even after the power of speech had departed, remained with his hands grasping the crucifix which his father Charles V. held when he was dying, and with his eyes fixed upon the altar of the church, till those eyes were closed in death.

All the other sights of the Escorial are of little importance compared with those which are connected with Philip II. One set of apartments was prettily decorated with inlaid woodwork by Charles IV. The endless corridors were once filled with fine pictures, now removed to Madrid. Only three of any consequence remain. In the chapter-house is a Velazquez of Jacob receiving from his elder sons the coat of Joseph; in the Refectory is a grand Last Supper of Titian; and in the Ante-Sacristia is a fine historical scene by Coello, representing the half-witted Charles II., with his court, upon their knees before the miraculous wafer, which bled at Gorcum, when trampled upon by Zwinglian heretics. Every Spanish sovereign is expected to make some offering to St. Laurence and the Escorial; that of Isabella II. was a gorgeous golden shrine for this very wafer, preserved behind the picture. The library contains several interesting pictures of kings, and some fine illuminated manuscripts. All the books are arranged with their backs to the wall.

Upon the south and east sides of the building

are so-called gardens—broad terraces with trim box edges, but on the whole possessing more architecture than vegetation. Here, from the angle of the terrace wall, one may best examine one of the external curiosities of the building, a glittering plaque of gold an inch thick and a yard square, which Philip II. built into the wall when the building was nearly complete, as a bravado to the world which expected it to become his ruin. Fortunately for its preservation it is near the top of the pyramid above the dome, where it glitters inaccessible, and reflects all the rays of the sun.

XII.

SEGOVIA AND AVILA.

AVILA, *May* 4.

IN a central situation in all the principal Spanish towns is an office ("Administracion") where you can not only take your railway ticket, but also tickets for a diligence to any town off the main line, from the station with which it is connected; and at the same time you can register your luggage through to your final destination. Here, in spite of many warnings from Madrid friends that we should be either blocked out by the snow, or carried off by the Carlists, we took our tickets for Segovia, and joined its diligence at the Vilalba station, an hour's journey from Madrid on the Northern Railway.

We had been quite unprepared for the magnificence of the Guadarrama mountains which we had to cross, and which are certainly more striking than even the Sierra Nevada. The ascent begins soon after leaving Vilalba, and is truly alpine, the road soon passing from the region of pines into that of snow, through which it had been cut, but which rose on either side in high walls, far above the top of the diligence, and, near the summit, to a height of fifteen feet. The descent was somewhat perilous, especially when we had to meet some heavily laden timber waggons in the narrow passage; but we reached the plains in safety, and, after traversing many miles of dismal country, saw Segovia rising against a faint pink sky, crowning a hill steep in itself, but from a distance scarcely seeming to rise above the level of the high surrounding uplands, from which it is separated by deep ravines. It is an especially Spanish scene, as you look upon the crowded town with its churches, towers, and red-roofed houses, piled one upon another, from a foreground of desolate moorland, where foaming mountain brooks dance and sparkle, through the pale grey rocks and burnt grass. Some old Romanesque churches occupy a rising ground to the right, and, as you turn the corner below them, you see the huge Roman aqueduct of Trajan striding across the hollow, and uniting the town with a populous

SEGOVIA.

suburb by its two tiers of arches. Beneath these you enter the main street of the city,—which winds up the hill beneath double gateways, and is full of interest from the beautiful ajimez windows which vary the surface of its mediæval houses,—into the principal square, all aflame with colour and costume, upon which the cathedral and the dark brown balconies of the wonderful old houses look grimly down.

If the reader will share our first walk in Segovia, he will descend with us to the aqueduct, which, like so many high bridges, the poor cheated Devil is said to have built in exchange for the soul of a fair Segoviana, who outwitted him by finding one stone missing in the work when she came to examine it. Turning to the left from hence, we are in the gorge, not bare, like that of Toledo, but bright with the fresh foliage of April. Here, nestling under the turfy slopes, are the Dominican convent and beautiful church of Santa Cruz, whose simple gothic nave is entered by a rich flamboyant portal well-deserving of attention; while the "Tanto-Monta" of Ferdinand and Isabella, with all their badges and devices, is formed into a graceful frieze under the roof.

Descending a steep path below the convent and

crossing a bridge, we enter a pretty alameda filled with willows and poplars, where the rushing river Eresma is perfectly lined by washerwomen, whose red and yellow dresses, gay as so many tulips, are reflected in its waters. While we are looking at them, one begins to sing, and the strain is taken up the whole way down the river bank, till the air rings with their choruses. It is now a verse from the Noche Buena, which tells how when the Virgin rested under an olive-tree during her flight into Egypt, the very leaves turned round to look at the newly-born one :—

> "La Virgen quiso sentarse
> A la sombra de un olivo
> Y las hojas se volvieron
> A ver al recien nacido."

Now a song more poetical in idea than in rhythm, which narrates how the Virgin laid aside her blue robe to wear mourning for her son :—

> "La Virgen se subió al cielo
> Y dejo su manto azul,
> Que cambió por uno negro
> Para el luto de Jesus."

At the end of the Alameda rises the great Geronymite monastery of El Parral, built in 1494 by the Marquis de Villena, in commemoration of a duel on its site, in which he overcame three antagonists at once. The building was gutted in the early Carlist wars, and has been closed since, but Don Ramón, the kindly old President of the Archæological Society, who spends much of his time there, invited us to pass the afternoon with him, and under his guidance we saw its numerous cloisters, its refectory with a richly wrought pulpit for the reader, its beautiful plateresque halls and staircase, its sacristia full of colour and picturesqueness, and, above all, its glorious church, abandoned and neglected, but still one of the most remarkable ecclesiastical buildings in Spain. It is entered from the west *under* the coro of 1494, which is like a wide gallery, with a beautiful Gothic rail of black marble. The carved stalls have been pulled down and carried off to San Francisco at Madrid, and many of the altars are removed, but the principal retablo remains, and is a grand work of Diego de Urbian in 1526. On either side of it stand the lofty plateresque monuments of the founder and his wife, and near the side door is the exquisite Gothic tomb of Doña Juana, daughter of King Ramiro of Leon. All this Don Ramón exhibited with the most kindly Spanish courtesy, illustrating it with a picturesque detail of legendary lore. The only part we could not admire was the room opening out of the cloister, which he had fitted up as a Pantheon, removing to it all the monuments of great citizens of Segovia from their rightful resting-places in the parish churches.

From El Parral, Don Ramón took us by a charming field walk to the Vera Cruz, built in 1204, by Honorius II., in imitation of the church of the Holy Sepulchre, which he had seen at Jerusalem. Around it rose the little town of Miraflores, but now all the houses have disappeared, and the old brown octagonal church, with its threefold apse and tall tower, stands forlorn and desolate on the barren rocks. In the interior is a raised chapel, occupying the upper story of what seems like a huge central pillar, and is supposed to indicate the site of the sepulchre. Two varieties of crosses mark its walls, for from "Messieurs les Templiers," said Don Ramón, it passed to " les Messieurs de S. Jean." A beautiful reliquary remains, which once contained a fragment of the true Cross brought by the founder.

Deeper in the valley, beyond Vera Cruz, is the great convent which contains the tutelar of Segovia,

Nuestra Señora de Fuencisla. From the abrupt cliff above it, criminals were thrown down, and a chapel and cypress mark the spot whence Santa Maria del Salto, a converted Jewess, took the fatal leap uninjured, when pushed over by her former co-religionists. Close by, the Eresma is joined by the mountain-brook Clamores, and from the narrow path which overhangs the river is the most striking view of the Alcazar, the magnificent castle in which the great Isabella took refuge, and whence she went forth to be proclaimed Queen of Castile. Here, in a great cave in the rock, live many poor homeless old men and women, who club together for their miserable subsistence, and sleep like wild beasts in this open-mouthed den. The smallest charity draws forth a shower of blessings, such as "God will pay your worship," "May God keep you and all your brothers," "May the Blessed Virgin walk with you in all your ways," and, from a blind man, "May Santa Lucia" (the patroness of eyes—she plucked out her own to preserve her virginity) "watch over the eyes of your worship."

We may ascend the hill by the Alcazar, but, alas! it now no longer contains anything to visit, for it was turned into a military college, and the students set fire to it and burnt it utterly in 1862, in the hope that they would thereby be moved to Madrid, and, what is worst of all, got off unpunished, being for the most part sons of high personages, and, in Spain, the poor only suffer the penalty of their misdeeds. It is now a mere shell of crumbling wall, but most picturesque. Constantly repeated in its decorations is the "Tanto Monta" of Ferdinand and Isabella, which is sometimes ascribed to the jealousy of Ferdinand, sometimes to their mutual affection. Not only the coin, but all their furniture and books were stamped with their devices, his being a yoke and hers a sheaf of arrows. It was common in married life, says Oviedo, for each party to take a device whose initial corresponded with that of the name of the other, as was the case with the "jùgo" and "flechas."

From the Alcazar, glancing at the noble tower of San Esteban, a few steps bring us to the cathedral, which, begun in 1525, is the last of the fine gothic cathedrals of Spain, and was built by the architects of Salamanca, of which it is partly a copy. In simplicity and general effect, the interior is perhaps unequalled in the Peninsula. Two cathedrals existed before this, and from the last of these, which stood close to the Alcazar, the present cloisters, which are amazingly lofty, were moved stone for stone. It was before the altar of the cathedral of Segovia, that Isabella the Catholic (Dec. 13, 1474) prostrated herself, after she had been declared Queen of Castile, and returning thanks to the Almighty for the protection hitherto afforded her, implored Him to enlighten her future counsels, that she might discharge the high trust reposed in her with equity and wisdom.

The last day of our all too short week at Segovia, we drove out six miles to San Ildefonso, where Philip V., in the last century, was charmed with a mountain grange while hunting, and built the palace of La Granja at a height of 3,840 feet, just under the snowy Guadarrama. In spite of the abuse in Ford and other guide-books, it is a most truly charming place, and the Alpine freshness, which lasts throughout the summer, and an excellent inn ("Europeo") with a French cuisine (oh, the relief from the oil and garlic of Spain!), render it additionally attractive. Long avenues lead up to a grille like that of the Place du Carrousel, whence you look down between lines of buildings appropriated to the ministers, the canons, and the offices of the court, to the palace itself, which is an old French château, in the style of Rambouillet, transported into the mountain-scenery of Spain. In the centre is the church where Philip V. and his queen are buried. Their apartments contain little of importance, but are hung with the beautiful silk embroidery which is to be seen in all the Spanish palaces, and are comfortable and attractive. Among the strange historical scenes which they have witnessed are the abdication of the founder in favour of his son Louis I., and his resumption of the crown, to which he was forced by his ambitious wife, on that son's death. Also they contain the little table at which Christina the Queen Regent was sitting when the three serjeants climbed in at the window, and forced her to sign her abdication.

There is an odd but picturesque contrast between the old château, with its pointed roofs and girouettes, standing in trim parterres of clipped yew and box, and the grand mountain-ranges behind, where the snow, perfectly pure and unbroken towards the summits, gradually meets and blends with the dark fir-woods. The intervening space is occupied by the so-called gardens, no cultivated flowers, but exquisite soft sylvan scenery, long avenues edged with holm-beech and shaded by tall oaks and elms, and endless little walks

PALACE OF LA GRANJA

winding through woods carpeted with violets and periwinkles—"Las Lagrimas de Jesu Christo," as the Spaniards poetically call them. In all the openings of the woods are statues, and fountains supplied by the fresh crystal streams which are seen in the distance falling in natural cascades from the high mountains; and, in front of the palace, is a great artificial waterfall, one sheet of silver, tumbling through the green woods, over a series of marble declivities, which perhaps will not bear detailed criticism, but whose general effect is one of great sylvan loveliness, of a mixture of art and nature which recalls the mythical ages of fauns and dryads, and the backgrounds of many old Italian pictures. Altogether, La Granja should on no account be unvisited, and the idler may be most happily idle there.

It is necessary to return to Vilalba to take tickets for Avila, which is a place far less known than it deserves, though it is on the central line of railway. As Spanish hotels go, the little inn of the "Dos de Majo" is excellent, and is kept by an Englishman and his daughter. On all sides the town is surrounded by a tawny desert, over whose arid plains numbers of grey boulders are scattered, like flocks of sheep. The circuit of the walls is complete, and so small, that most, even of the mediæval buildings, are outside it. These comprise a wonderful collection of churches of the greatest interest to the archæologist. San Vicente, founded 313, contains a thirteenth century shrine of that saint, who was not the famous deacon of Zaragoza, but another of the same name, also martyred under Dacian, because he stamped upon an altar of Jupiter and left the marks of his feet there. His body was guarded by a serpent, which attacked a rich Jew who came to mock at it, and made him vow to build this church if he escaped with his life. Like the Bocca della Verità at Rome, the hole out of which the snake came was long a spot for adjuration, he who took the oath putting his hand into it, so that the snake (which did attack Bishop Vilches under these circumstances in 1458) might bite him if he swore falsely.

Following the outside of the walls from hence, we reach a tiny Romanesque church on the river side, standing in a little weedy enclosure with three stone crosses. It is always closed now, and in spite of the disagreeable extortionate Cerberus who guards it, the keys must be obtained, for the sake of seeing the beautiful touching monument of its patron, the bishop San Segundo. He is said to have pushed a Moor over the battlements of the neighbouring tower with his own hands, a deed of prowess which will always render him popular as a Spanish saint, but which does not seem consistent with the expression of his penitent kneeling figure rapt in an ecstasy of prayer.

Another glorious monument is that, in San Tomas, of Prince Juan, only son of Ferdinand and Isabella. The church in which he is buried was one of the favourite foundations of the Catholic sovereigns, who frequently resided in the palace-convent which is attached to it. It was in one of the rooms which may still be seen in this building, that Isabella was induced to give her written sanction to the proceedings of the Inquisition. Here also she devoted herself to the education of Prince Juan, heir of the united Spanish monarchies. Ten youths, selected from the sons of the chief nobles, were brought to reside with him in the palace, five of his own age and five older, that emulation might stimulate him to greater diligence in his studies; and a mimic council was formed to deliberate on matters of government and public policy, over which the prince presided, in order that he might be early initiated into his important future duties. A brilliant scholar, an accomplished linguist and musician, beautiful in person, and endowed with the most amiable, generous, and winning of characters, he grew up the delight of his parents, and the idol of their people. In March, 1497, being then in his twentieth year, he was married at Burgos to Margaret, daughter of the Emperor Maximilian, with whom he had every prospect of happiness. As soon as his marriage festivities were concluded, he retired with his bride to Salamanca, while his parents proceeded to be present at another marriage, that of their daughter Isabella to the king of Portugal, at Valencia de Alcantara. While there, they received the news of the alarming illness of their son. Ferdinand hastened with all possible speed to his side, leaving Isabella to follow by slower stages. When he arrived, the Prince was dying. At first the unhappy father strove to cheer him with hopes he could not himself feel, but Juan checked him, telling him that he could not be deceived, that he was prepared to leave a world which at the best was filled with vanity and trouble, and that his only prayer was that his parents might be able to feel the same resignation which he himself experienced. He died October 4, 1497, before Isabella could arrive. Great alarm was felt as to the effect which the terrible tidings might have upon her, but she evinced the same fortitude which sustained her in every other adversity, and the young Prince's tutor, Peter Martyr, records that she only replied to the fatal intelligence in the words of Scripture— "The Lord hath given, the Lord hath taken away, blessed be His name!"

The exquisite sleeping figure of Prince Juan, the most touching of sepulchral effigies, lies with folded hands, and features smiling in death, upon a marble altar-tomb. The coro, which is placed above an elliptical arch at the western entrance, still retains the two splendidly carved stalls, which his parents ever afterwards occupied at mass, close to the gallery rail, that they might look down meanwhile upon the image of their child. They were dressed in sackcloth, which was substituted in this great calamity for the white serge hitherto worn as royal mourning; and Peter Martyr vividly describes how, as they sate, the eyes of one would seek those of the other, and cause a fresh outburst of grief—though, he adds, they would "cease to be human, and would have been harder than adamant, had they not felt what they had lost."

With the extraordinary disregard of historical

relics which prevails in Spain, the rough boys of the town were allowed, till a few years ago, to come into this deserted church at will, and amuse themselves by breaking off and selling the delicate ornaments of the tomb. It is wonderful that the figure itself should remain uninjured. Now it is protected by a coarse deal railing. Near that of their master, in a side chapel, is the beautiful tomb of his favourite attendants, Juan Davila and Juana Velazquez. The cloisters, courts, and staircases, rich with ball-flower ornament, remain, though unused and neglected, the same as when they witnessed the heart-broken grief of their founders.

The other churches of Avila are so interesting that one seems to have no enthusiasm left for the cathedral. Yet it is exceedingly curious, being more than half a fortress, built by Garcia de Estrella in 1107. Its eastern apse, projecting over the city wall, is machicolated and fortified like a castle. In its high tower storks build, and stand undisturbed for hours on the top of its pinnacles, as if they were petrified there, their beautiful white plumage glittering against the deep blue sky. The interior is very impressive, with tall dark gothic arches, and glorious stained windows. The retablo, of the time of Ferdinand and Isabella, has pictures by Berreguete and Borgoña.

The streets of Avila are full of very curious old houses, perfectly unchanged from mediæval times. In the courtyard of one of them are several of the extraordinary stone pigs, called Toros de Guisando, which are believed to have been idols of the primitive inhabitants. A few houses are richly decorated and very magnificent. But the greater part, even of the oldest and noblest families, are of most simple character. The general arrangement is the same. Over the entrance is a huge sculptured shield of arms, generally much stained by weather and gilded by lichen. Above it projects a stone balcony almost always occupied by some of the pet quails, which make the air resound with their strange cry, and which are great favourites all over the north of Spain, where they are called *reclamos*, being taken out by sportsmen, when their cry, always incessant, attracts others of the same breed.

The principal entrance leads into a vast hall, on either side of which are large doors opening into chambers which are never used except in the great events of a human life, a birth, a marriage, or a burial. On the opposite side of the hall is another door which communicates with the body of the house (Cuerpo de casa), and facing it a door leading to a gallery which opens upon a spacious yard, in which are the bakehouse, the oven, the hay-lofts, in short all the domestic offices, with a separate entrance. On either side of this door, in the " Cuerpo di casa," are two great chambers, one being the kitchen of the masters, the other that of the servants. In the first, in which no cooking takes place, and which might more properly be called a dining-hall, is an enormous chimney, whose opening occupies the whole face of one wall. Here in winter a huge fire is perpetually burning, in which whole trees are consumed. On either side low benches covered with wool cushions are fixed against the walls. In holes made in the walls, called *vasares*, are symmetrically arranged large vases full of water; besides these are displayed on shelves a collection of *bucares* (a peculiar drinking jug) of different sizes and shapes. In the tiled kitchen of the servants all the work of the house is done. On either side of the " Cuerpo di casa " are the doors of the dwelling rooms, which generally look upon a garden supplied with a few flowers, a great many medicinal herbs, and some vegetables. These inner chambers generally have glass windows, whilst the rooms which look upon the streets have only shutters.

In a house of this kind, in one of the fashionable streets in Avila, was born, March 28, 1515, Doña Teresa de Cepede, who was destined to be the most extraordinary woman of her age and country, and who is not unnaturally regarded by Roman Catholics as having been raised up, together with St. Ignatius Loyola, to give new life to their religion, in the sixteenth century, when it was suffering so much from the inroads of Protestantism. Her father, Don Alphonso Sanchez de Cepede, was a man of most virtuous and holy life, her mother Doña Beatrix Ahumada, was also pious, but, quaintly adds her historian, "was too much given to reading romances." The tendencies of both were repeated in their daughter Teresa, who was one of twelve children. In her earliest childhood she was devoted to reading the lives of the saints and martyrs, and at eight years old escaped from home, and was captured by her uncle, setting off with her little brother Rodrigo to the land of the Moors, in the hope of being martyred by them. What affected these children most in their reading, was that the happiness of the blessed was for ever the punishment of the damned for ever.—" *For* ever," they used to exclaim, clasping each other's little hands, and looking in each other's faces, "*for ever!*" Their great desire was to become hermits, and they tried to build for themselves little hermitages in the garden, which they never were able to finish.

Upon her mother's death, when she was twelve years old, Teresa got possession of her library of novels, which are said greatly to have perverted her mind, and filled her with the desire of admiration and thought of her personal appearance. Her father became so alarmed at the change in her, that he placed her for a time in the Augustinian convent at Avila, where she was at first perfectly miserable, but became reconciled by the kindness and protection of a devout nun, who never ceased to bring before her, with meaning views, the text, "Many are called, but few chosen." This so worked upon her vanity, that she determined to become a nun, and, though her father absolutely refused his consent, took the veil in the Carmelite convent of Avila in her twentieth year.

Here for twenty years her mind was never at rest. "On one side," she writes, "I was called as it were by God, on the other I was tempted by regrets for the world. I wished to combine my aspirations towards heaven with my earthly sympathies, and I found that this was impossible; I fell—I rose, only to fall again; I had neither the peaceful satisfaction of a soul reconciled with God, nor could I taste the pleasures which the world offered me. . . . At length God had pity upon me. I read in the temptations of St. Augustine how he was tried and tempted, and how at length he conquered." The difficulties of Teresa in a religious life were increased, partly by her ill-health, and partly by the lax rules of the convent, which allowed her to receive constant visits from secular and worldly persons. Thus, after she had been persuaded by her confessor, no longer to be content with vocal devotion, but constantly to converse with God in mental prayer, and when through the force of prayer her character became changed, it was the first object of her heart to save others from the dangers to which she had been herself exposed in a religious life, and to bring about a reform of the Carmelite Order. Assisted by the inhabitants of her native place, she founded a new convent at Avila, which she dedicated to St. Joseph, and, upon its success, proceeded to found in turn seventeen convents for women and fifteen for men in different towns of Spain. These she usually began to build with scarcely any funds whatever. It is narrated of her that she arrived at Toledo to found a convent with only four ducats, and that, when people remonstrated, she said, "Teresa and four ducats can do nothing, but God, Teresa, and four ducats can do anything." Unhappily the mortifications she imposed upon herself, the constant state of self-meditation in which she lived, and the flatteries of the priests who surrounded her, worked her mind into a state of religious enthusiasm which bordered upon insanity. At one time she affirmed that an angel, in corporeal form, had pierced her through the bowels with a tangible dart tipped with fire to inflame them with the love of God. At another time, while repeating the hymn "Veni Creator Spiritus," she believed that she heard a voice from heaven announcing to her that she should no more hold conversation with men but with angels. She was frequently in a state of ecstasy, in which her body is believed to have been lifted from the ground, while her voice held communion with invisible spirits.

Gradually, however, as years grew upon her, these mystic fancies seem to have cleared away, leaving her with the simplicity and truth of a mind purified by prayer. She used to say that "Our

Lord is a great lover of humility because He is the great lover of truth, and humility is a certain truth, by which we know how little we are, and that we have no good of ourselves." Speaking of the succours she received from the world in her various undertakings, she said, "I perceive clearly that they are all no better than so many twigs of dried rosemary, and that there is no leaning upon them : for upon the least weight of contradiction pressing upon them, they are presently broken. I have learned this by experience, that the true remedy against our falling is to lean on the Cross, and to trust only in Him who was fastened to it."

Teresa lived till her sixty-eighth year. As her health became feebler she wrote, "It seems to me there is no reason why I should live except to suffer, and accordingly this is what I ask with most earnestness from my God. Sometimes I say to Him with my whole heart, 'Lord, either to die or to suffer, I ask nothing else for myself.' It comforts me also to hear the clock strike ; for so methinks I draw a little nearer to the seeing of God, since one hour more of my life is passed." She was seized with her last illness in the house of the Duchess of Alva, but was moved to her own convent at Avila, where she died October 4, 1582, her last words being those of the Miserere, "A broken and a contrite heart, O God, thou wilt not despise."

She has left many written works—some for the guidance of her nuns, others addressed to the whole Catholic Church. The great object of them all is to enforce the importance and power of prayer, both active and passive. Love—the love of God—was the mainspring of her every idea. Hell, she only thought of as the place where there is no love." Of Satan she said, "Poor wretch, he cannot love." Among her many passionate out-pourings is one

"To Jesus Christ, Crucified.

"That which makes me love Thee, my God, is not the heaven which Thou hast promised me; nor is it the hell full of terrors which makes me desire not to offend Thee.

"That which influences me is Thine own self, O God; that which influences me is the sight of Thee upon the cross, nailed and insulted! That which influences me is the sight of the wounds in Thy body, of the pangs of Thy death.

"Thy love, in fact, is what influences me; and to such a degree that I could love Thee all the same if there were no heaven; and if there were no hell I would fear Thee no less.

"Give me nothing in return for this my love for Thee; for were I not to hope what I am longing for I should love Thee as well as I do now."

Mrs. Jameson truly observes that "what was strong, beautiful, true, and earnest, was in Teresa herself; what was morbid, miserable, and mistaken was the result of the influences around her."

In her convent at Avila the nuns never now sit in the stalls during mass, but only upon the steps, because they believe that when Teresa was present, the stalls were occupied by angels. In the adjoining chapel is her shrine, occupying the spot where Bishop Yepez relates that as she was about to receive the communion from Bishop Mendoza, she was lifted from the ground in a rapture, higher than the gates, through which (according to the custom in nunneries) the Sacrament was to be given to her, and clinging to the rails, prayed, "Lord, suffer not, for such a favour, a wicked woman to pass for virtuous," after which she was permitted to descend. In the garden is an apple-tree, planted by Teresa, whose fruit is supposed to be good for every species of female disorder.

XIII.

SALAMANCA, VALLADOLID, AND BURGOS.

IT is a long tedious journey by diligence from Avila to Salamanca. We left Avila at midnight, guided by lanthorns down the tortuous streets from the hotel to the place where the diligence was waiting to be packed, amid much vociferation of greedy porters, and whining of the innumerable beggars, who are quite as alert by night as by day, if there is a chance of a stranger falling a prey to them. It was a bitterly cold night (May 5th), and the wind poured cruelly in through the many cracks in the rackety old berlina as we traversed the hideous, arid, treeless plains, which even the pale moonlight failed to beautify. Day broke, and hour after hour passed wearily on, till about ten A.M. came the welcome sight of a bright yellow cathedral and town rising on the horizon, and we soon began to skirt the blue river Tormes which flows beneath its walls.

Salamanca once possessed twenty-five colleges, twenty-five churches, twenty-five convents, twenty-five professors, and twenty-five arches of its bridge; but the last alone remain intact,—colleges, churches, convents, and professorships have alike fallen; their destruction, begun by the French, having been finished by the law, which was made for the sake of plunder under Queen Isabella II., that no corporate body could hold any property. The university, which boasted above ten thousand students in the fourteenth century, has now little more than one thousand, and the splendid collegiate buildings, palaces worthy of the Corso of Rome or the Grand Canal of Venice, are either in ruins or let out to poor families, with the exception of San Bartolomé, which is turned into the house of the civil governor, and El Arzobisbo, whose beautiful *cinque-cento* buildings are now given up to the Irish college. This formerly was situated in another part of the town: it contains only nine students now, but the original foundation was magnificent, and bore witness to the anxiety of its founder Philip II. to spite his sister-in-law Elizabeth of England. Day by day

Salamanca becomes more entirely a city of ruins, and presents much the same appearance which Oxford would do were its revenues all stolen by the Government, and Christ-Church, Merton, Magdalen, University, &c., abandoned to the rats and owls. The few students who remain are lodged in private houses in the town, and go up for their " classes " to the building of the University proper, which answers to that called "the Schools" at Oxford, and has a gorgeous plateresque front and a curious Convocation House. The little square behind it, surrounded by collegiate buildings, is much like one of our college "quads." In its centre is a statue of the ecclesiastical poet Fra Luiz de Leon, who is numbered with Cervantes, Saarvedra, and Cardinal Ximenes amongst the eminent students of the University. The Library contains many original letters of his, together with a splendid collection of MSS., chiefly brought from confiscated monasteries, and a large number of printed books of the fifteenth century. A volume of the Lord's Prayer in one hundred and fifty-seven languages, ordered by the first Napoleon, is exhibited with great pride by the librarian. The Reading-room is used by natives of Salamanca to a degree which shames the more populous Oxford;

SALAMANCA.

a day seldom passes without as many as ninety students availing themselves of it.

The university buildings face the cathedral, which was begun in 1513. Its florid Gothic is excessively rich in detail, but wanting in general effect, and the brilliant yellow colour of its stone annuls all appearance of antiquity: the interior, however, would be exceedingly magnificent, if it were not so sadly blocked up by the coro. In one of the chapels the Musarabic ritual has been continued, as at Toledo. A few pictures deserve notice, especially those by Luiz de Morales, who here merits his epithet of " the Spanish Perugino," and those by the rare master Fernando Gallegos, who was a native of Salamanca, where he died in 1550. From the north aisle one passes into a second and older cathedral, built in 1102 by the famous Bishop Geronimo, the confessor of the Cid, who fought by his side in all his battles, and supported his dead body in its final ride from Valencia to San Pedro de Cerdeña. He is buried here, and above his tomb hung for five hundred years "El Christo de las Batallas," the famous bronze crucifix of the Cid, which he always carried with him. This has now disappeared, and is not to be found even in the Relicario, but the canons know of the hiding-place, where, in this age of church-robbery, it has been secreted. The tomb of Geronimo was opened in 1606, when it is affirmed that the body of the holy warrior smelt truly delicious. The retablo, which follows the curved form of the apse in the old cathedral, contains a number of paintings interesting from the poetical character of their subjects. In that on—" Angels came and ministered to Him "—a table-cloth spread with food is held by several angels before the Saviour in the wilderness, while others kneeling present fruit and a cup of wine. The exterior of this church is half a fortress, and gave it the epithet of "Fortis Salamantina:" the vaulted lanthorn has a low crocketed spire and a scalloped stone roof.

From the cathedral, San Esteban is approached by the Calle del Colon, a memorial of Christopher Columbus and his residence in the neighbouring Dominican convent, whose friars under Deza the Inquisitor upheld him and his scheme, when the doctors of the university found it to be "vain, impracticable, and resting on grounds too weak to merit the support of government." In gratitude for the hospitalities he received from the Dominicans, Columbus used the first virgin gold imported from the New World in gilding the retablo of their church, and most gorgeous is still its appearance, as seen from under the dark elliptical arch of the coro, through which the church is entered with such effect, leaving the view unbroken towards the high-altar—as at El Parral, and San Tomas of Avila.. The western exterior is a labyrinth of plateresque gothic decoration, like that of the university.

In the little convent of Las Duenas close by, Santa Teresa had one of her famous visions, when she came hither to found the convent of her own Order outside the gates. In this and all the other convents of Salamanca, the nuns are now reduced to a state of absolute starvation. The principal of their dowries, which according to rule was given by their parents in the same way in which a marriage portion is bestowed, was confiscated by the government of Isabella, and the interest, which they were promised during their lives, has never been paid by that of Amadeo. It has been necessary to make collections at the church doors in order to supply these unfortunate ladies with bread. While the nuns have been left to starve, the conventual buildings of the monks have for the most part been pulled down, to the destruction of many precious architectural memorials. Even the splendid decorations of the windows and staircases have been sold for the value of the material, aristocratic families refusing to purchase them, from the fear of being supposed to recognise, even in the most distant way, these acts of vandalism. Great indeed is the fall of religious bodies in Spain!—only forty years ago the Dominicans of Salamanca had relays of mules constantly running between their town and Santander, in order that they might have their fish constantly fresh from the sea.

The Plaza Mayor, surrounded by arcaded galleries, has the reputation of being the finest square in Spain, but is surrounded by shops such as the back streets of Bermondsey and Whitechapel would be ashamed of, and by day wears a most forlorn and deserted appearance. In the evening all the few remaining students congregate there and enliven it a little, marching up and down proudly in their ragged cloaks, arm-in-arm, and puffing their eternal cigarritos. There is no place where pride in rags is so splendidly exhibited as at Salamanca.] Madame d'Aulnois narrates that one day looking out of a window, she saw a woman selling small pieces of fresh salmon and calling upon all the passers-by to buy of her. A poor shoemaker came and asked for a pound of her salmon. "You do not hesitate about the price," she said, "because you think it is cheap, but you are mistaken, it costs a crown the pound." The shoemaker, insulted at her doubting him, said in an angry tone, "If it had been cheap, one pound would have been enough for me, but, since it is dear, I wish for three"—and he immediately gave her three crowns and walked away twirling his moustache and glowering at the spectators, though the three crowns were all that he had in the world, the earnings of his whole week, and the next day he, his wife, and his little children would fast on something less than bread and water. This was in 1643; but Spain never changes, and scenes of the same character might be witnessed any day in Salamanca. It is the want of regard for this Spanish amour-propre which makes the generality of English travellers so unpopular in Spain. Théophile Gautier narrates that an Englishman travelling from Seville to Xeres, not understanding that a distinction of classes was unknown at such times, sent his driver to dine in the kitchen of the inn where they halted. The driver, who in his heart thought that he would have been doing great honour to a heretic by sitting at the same table with him, concealed his indignation at the time, but in the middle of the road, three or four leagues from Xeres, in a horrible desert full of bogs and brambles, pushed the Englishman out of the carriage, and cried out, as he whipped on his horse, " My Lord, you did not find me worthy to sit at your table ; and I, Don Jose Balbino Bustamente y Orozco, find you too bad company to occupy a seat in my carriage. Good night."

Travellers in early spring will observe the quantities of pet lambs in the streets of Salamanca, generally decorated with bunches of red worsted. By a curious custom a general slaughter of these takes place on Good Friday upon the doorsteps— the little creatures being executed by their own mistresses, who stab them in the throat.

The inn at Salamanca, La Burgalesca, is quite excellent, and is kept by very honest deserving people, so that in the dearth of good inns in the Peninsula, it forms a great attraction to the place.

A woeful drive of six hours across a barren wilderness brought us from Salamanca to Zamora. No single object of interest varied the monotony of the way, except a stork's nest on a low campanile in a village we passed through, on which the mother stood imperturbably feeding her young, while the heavy diligence rolled by, almost within reach. At length, beyond the Douro, rose, on a steep though low hillside, the houses and churches of Zamora, ending on the left in the cathedral, which is of most mosque-like appearance, and we entered the town by a long low gate-defended bridge of seventeen pointed arches.

There is no inn in Zamora, and it is almost impossible to obtain any food there. Nothing could we find except bon-bons and some very aged sponge-cakes, so that before evening hunger fairly drove us away. There is not much to see. One long narrow street winds along the heights—passing on the way the interesting little Romanesque church of La Magdalena, and a dusty alameda planted with coronella—to the cathedral, which is of the twelfth century, with a curious dome, much like that of the old cathedral at Salamanca. The coro contains a beautiful carved lectern, and is surrounded with magnificent stall-work decorated by figures of Old Testament saints, bearing scrolls with legends referring to our Lord. There are some interesting tombs. From the little platform below the cathedral is a striking view upon the Douro rushing immediately beneath the rocks upon which it is built, and then over the wide desolate Africa-like plains broken only by boulders of grey rock. We sate down to draw upon the steep bank above the river, but our doing so in time of Carlist alarms excited quite a commotion in the city, and we were soon pounced upon by a policeman and carried off, followed by a mob of people, for examination, but our passports proving satisfactory, we were speedily released.

The Carlist troubles were now at their climax, and as the railway to the Asturias was cut in twenty-five places, we were reluctantly compelled to give up for the time visiting that most interesting corner of Spain, and also the cathedral of Leon. We were not even able to linger at Toro and its curious colegiata, but hastened on to the safer Valladolid. We joined the main-line of railway at Medina del Campo, but it was too dark to see its curious walls. Here the great Isabella died, November 26, 1504. Hence, on the day of her death, Peter Martyr wrote to the Archbishop of Granada, "My hand falls powerless by my side for very sorrow. The world has lost its noblest ornament; a loss to be deplored not only by

Spain, which she has so long carried forward in the career of glory, but by every nation in Christendom; for she was the mirror of every virtue, the shield of the innocent, and an avenging sword to the wicked. I know none of her sex, in ancient or modern times, who, in my judgment, is at all to be named with this incomparable woman."

It was midnight when we reached Valladolid and were guided by a boy through the long dark alameda of the Campo Grande, and up the wide streets to our inn.

Valladolid, which was the capital of Castile under Juan II., and one of the most flourishing cities of Spain under Charles V. and Philip II., has been a mere wreck of its former self since the French invasion, in which many of its most important buildings were destroyed. Its situation is dreary in the extreme, in a barren dusty plain quite devoid of natural beauty. Two small rivers, the Pisuerga and the Esqueva, meet under its walls and water its flat ugly gardens. The great Plaza is vast and imposing; the cathedral, the work of Herrera (1585), is imposing too, and grand in its outlines, but intensely bare and cold. Near it stands the beautiful church of Santa Maria l'Antigua, with a picturesque western steeple of the twelfth century and a ruined cloister, and there are several other churches where the architect will find interesting *bits*. All travellers, however, should visit San Pablo, a Dominican convent rebuilt in 1463 by Cardinal Torquemada, who had been one of its monks and was the ferocious confessor of Isabella the Catholic, from whom he extorted a promise that she would devote herself " to the extirpation of heresy for the glory of God and the exaltation of the Catholic faith." Under his influence *Autos da fé* frequently took place in the Plaza Mayor of Valladolid, attended by the Court then, as bull-fights have been in late years, and in which the victims were arrayed in yellow shirts painted with flames and figures of devils. Torquemada, however, was also a great patron of art and literature, and the inscription " Operibus credite," in reference to the splendour of the buildings which he founded here, was repeated round his tomb. This monument was destroyed by the French, but the façade of San Pablo is still a miracle of labyrinthine gothic tracery quite splendid of its kind, and so is the neighbouring façade of San Gregorio, founded in 1488 by Bishop Alonzo of Burgos. Close by is the curious old house in which Philip II. was born.

The Museo must be visited, for, though its upper story is filled with atrocious rubbish, pictorial art in wood is nowhere so well represented as in the collection of figures which occupies the ground floor. The best of these are from the hands of the violent Juan de Juni, remarkable for his knowledge of anatomy when it was generally unknown in Spain, or from those of the gentle Gregorio Hernandez (1566—1636), who, like Fra Angelico and Juanes, devoted himself to religious subjects, and never began to work without preparing his mind by prayer. At the end of the principal gallery, which is surrounded by the beautiful choir stalls of San Benito, are the splendid bronze effigies of the Duke and Duchess of Lerma, by Pompeio Leoni, removed from San Pablo.

We were at Valladolid on Ascension Day, upon which, at the hour of mass, all the leaves upon the trees are supposed to fold themselves one upon the other in the form of the Cross, out of very devotion and reverence.

Terribly hot in the height of summer, we found Valladolid insupportably cold in the middle of May, and were glad to hurry on to Burgos, where, however, the climate was even more Siberian.

From being the first place generally visited in Spain, Burgos has been greatly overrated by most travellers. It is not a picturesque place, and its new houses and white quays along the banks of the Arlanzon have the look of a very inferior Bordeaux. A fine old gateway is jammed in between insignificant modern buildings, and even the cathedral is so hemmed in that it is difficult to obtain any good near view of the exterior. As Burgos is on the high-road, and almost all foreigners halt there, the innkeepers are more extortionate than elsewhere, and it is necessary to make a very strict bargain on entering the hotels.

We spent the whole of our first day at Burgos in an excursion to the tomb of the Cid, from which travellers are strangely dissuaded by Murray's hand-book, but which is exceedingly curious and interesting. The road follows a long alameda by the banks of the Arlanzon for about two miles, and then ascends a hill to the convent of Miraflores, which looks at a distance as Eton chapel would look if placed on a bare wind-stricken height. The church and convent were completed in 1488 by Isabella the Catholic in memory of her father Juan II., and her beloved mother Isabella, to whom she was so tenderly attached that she insisted on

ARCO DE SANTA MARIA, BURGOS.

making it a condition of her marriage settlement that her husband should always treat her mother with proper respect. Their gorgeous alabaster monument by Gil de Siloe stands before the high altar, and is perhaps the most perfectly glorious tomb in the world. On one side is another beautiful monument to their son Alonzo, whose early death conferred the crown upon Isabella. The convent is almost deserted now, only three monks remain, tottering with old age, and so poor that they with difficulty find any soup to give to the still more wretched beggars who hover round their gates.

It is a most desolate drive from hence to San Pedro de Cerdeña, the beloved home of the Cid, whither he desired that he might be taken with his last breath. There is no road, but a mere track marked by stones across the sweeping platforms of the hill-tops, covered with burnt yellow turf which took fine effects of colour in the shifting lights and shadows of a showery day. More and more desolate does the country become: not a tree, not even the smallest shrub is to be seen, till you reach the edge of a hollow in the hills, where the vast monastery of San Pedro rises in a grim solitude, backed by jagged purple mountains with snow-covered tops. As a first or a last view in Spain, nothing can be more characteristic of the fallen grandeur of the country in its splendid ruin.

Over the gate of the palace convent stands the mutilated figure of the Cid on horseback riding over the prostrate Moors. The building is massive and solemn to a degree, but almost entirely deserted. A woman and a filthy priest are its only inhabitants. The priest herds his pigs through the greater part of the day, and in the early morning he says mass in the grand conventual church. "Have you any congregation?" we asked. "Only the woman," he replied.

Across a courtyard overgrown with nettles, the priest led us to the tomb of the Cid, which was erected by Alonzo el Sabio in 1272. It occupies the centre of a chapel, surrounded by the shields of his friends and followers. On the high altar tomb are the effigies of the Cid and his faithful wife Ximena, whom on his death-bed he commended to the care of One mightier than himself, with the oft-repeated words, "God has promised." Around his tomb rest in peace, his son, his two daughters, Elvira, Queen of Navarre, and Maria Sol, Queen of Arragon, with their husbands, and his principal chieftains; but the Cid's own body has been carried off to Burgos, where it is preserved in a wooden box in the town-hall! Around the tomb is the epitaph,—

> "Belliger, invictus, famosus marte triumphis,
> Clauditur hoc tumulo magnus Didaci Rodericus."

The Cid is so well known by his appellation of the sheikh or chieftain, that his own name Rodrigo Ruy Diaz is scarcely remembered. His story is, however, better preserved than that of any other person of his time, his deeds of war which made him so terrible to his enemies, and his many deeds of generosity and kindness to his friends, the poor, and the Church, having been handed down in a hundred ballads and mediæval romances. With him, almost all the chroniclers mention his faithful steed Bavieca, which was present at his death-bed, and wept great tears over his dying master. Upon it, the dead body of the Cid was borne hither from Valencia, held upright in his armour, and with his good sword Tisona fixed firmly in his hand, with which, says the legend, he, though dead, knocked down a Jew who audaciously plucked him by the beard. Here, near his master, Bavieca is buried, under a mound shaded by two elm-trees, according to the will of the Cid, who wrote, "When ye bury Bavieca, dig deep, for shameful thing it were, that he should be eaten by curs, who hath trampled down so much currish flesh of Moors."

It was his hatred of the Moors which first attracted the Cid to the convent of San Pedro, where, in 872, two hundred monks were massacred by the Moor Zephe, monks from whose holy bodies blood always issued afresh on the anniversary of their execution. This miracle was confirmed as authentic by Pope Sixtus IV. in 1473, and, though some heretics affirm that it afterwards ceased, the priest who shows the convent evidently believes that it is still in full force, and marvels that his visitors should find the tomb of a warrior more interesting than the gaudy shrine of such sanguineous martyrs.

There is nothing to be told of the vast cathedral of Burgos, which has not been already narrated by O'Shea and by the original Ford. It is tremendous in size, beautiful in parts, but never, I think, very striking as a whole. Some distance out of Burgos, in an opposite direction from Miraflores, near the green avenues of the Arlanzon, is the beautiful convent of Las Huelgas, founded for the Cistercians by the wife of Alonzo VIII., Eleanor of England, daughter of Henry II., and sister of Richard Cœur de Lion. Through the grille which divides its splendid church, you look upon the choir, whose stalls, during service-time, are occupied by picturesque white robed Cistercian nuns—a beautiful picture which remains stamped upon the mind long after that of the arches and pillars has faded away.

The railway from Burgos to the Bidassoa passes through Vittoria and St. Sebastian, but except the latter, which generally forms an excursion from Biarritz, offers nothing which need arrest a traveller, beyond the manners and proverbs of the Basque population, and their language, which an old Basque woman assured one of our friends was not only the best, but by far the oldest language in the world—in fact it was that which Adam and Eve spoke in Paradise. As we sped along, the banks of the railway were constantly occupied by the picturesque Carlist troops, and, at many of the principal stations, Carlist regiments were drawn up, in their scarlet Basque caps and sashes, but offered us no annoyance. We arrived safely at Irun, and there took leave of Spain, with the feeling that great and frequent as had been the discomforts of our travels there, in the afterglow only the rosy tints would predominate and the annoyances fade into shadow. Here also I will

T

take leave of my reader, with the expression which a Spanish traveller knows better than any other—with which every passer-by salutes him, with which every beggar wishes him farewell—" Vaya Usted con Dios."

THE END.

www.ingramcontent.com/pod-product-compliance
Lightning Source LLC
Chambersburg PA
CBHW030732230426
43667CB00007B/689